Lea & Perrins

Appetizer, Soup, Main Dish, Vegetable, and Salad COOKBOOK

The Supermarket Book Company

Photograph & Recipe Development
by Louis & Neale, Inc.
Empire State Building
New York, N.Y. 10001

Copyright © 1975 by Ridge Press/Rutledge Books, ,

The Benjamin Company, Inc., and Lea & Perrins, Inc.

This supermarket edition produced by Rutledge Books

Published by The Supermarket Book Company

For further information, contact
The Benjamin Company, Inc.
485 Madison Avenue
New York, N.Y. 10021

Library of Congress Catalog Card Number 74-18140

Printed in the United States of America

STARTERS AND SNACKS

Tasty appetizers to begin a meal,

to munch between meals

WORCESTERED NUTS AND BOLTS

5 cups

1 tablespoon butter or
   margarine
2 tablespoons Lea & Perrins
   Worcestershire Sauce

2 cups salted peanuts
2 cups toasted oat cereal
1 cup pretzel sticks

In a large saucepan melt butter. Stir in Lea & Perrins. Add peanuts, cereal, and pretzels; toss to coat. Spread evenly over the bottom of a shallow baking pan. Bake in a preheated very hot oven (450 F.) until hot and golden brown, about 8 minutes. Serve warm or cold. Store in a tightly covered container.

AVOCADO DUNK

about 1 cup

1 ripe avocado
2 teaspoons Lea & Perrins
   Worcestershire Sauce

1 teaspoon lemon juice
½ teaspoon Tabasco pepper
   sauce

Mash avocado. Add Lea & Perrins, lemon juice, and Tabasco; mix well. Chill. Serve with shrimp or chips.

EMPANADAS
(Argentine Beef Turnovers)

about 4 dozen

1 package (8 oz.) cream cheese, softened
½ cup butter or margarine, softened
1½ cups all-purpose flour
1 tablespoon olive or salad oil
2 tablespoons minced onion
½ pound ground lean beef
1 can (8¼ oz.) tomatoes, drained and crushed
2 tablespoons chopped raisins
2 tablespoons chopped pitted green olives
1 tablespoon Lea & Perrins Worcestershire Sauce
½ teaspoon salt
½ teaspoon oregano leaves, crumbled
1 hard-cooked egg, chopped
1 egg yolk
1 tablespoon water
¼ cup sesame seed

In the large bowl of an electric mixer blend cream cheese and butter. Gradually add flour; blend until dough is smooth. Divide dough into 3 balls; cover and chill until firm, about 30 minutes. In a medium skillet heat oil. Add onion; sauté for 3 minutes. Add meat; cook and stir until browned, about 5 minutes. Stir in tomatoes, raisins, olives, Lea & Perrins, salt, and oregano. Simmer, uncovered, for 5 minutes, stirring occasionally. Stir in chopped egg; cool. On a lightly floured board roll each ball of dough separately to ⅛-inch thickness. With a 3-inch biscuit cutter, cut out circles. Spoon about 1 teaspoon of the meat mixture onto one side of each circle. Moisten edges with water; fold pastry over filling to form a semicircle; press edges to seal; crimp with fork tines. Repeat. Prick tops of turnovers to allow steam to escape. Mix egg yolk with water; brush over tops of turnovers. Sprinkle with sesame seed. Place on cookie sheets. Bake in a preheated hot oven (400 F.) until golden, about 12 minutes. Serve hot.

6

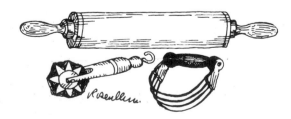

Opposite: *Empañadas*

BACON "NUTS"

about 2 dozen

¼ cup Lea & Perrins
    Worcestershire Sauce
1 teaspoon salt
1 teaspoon lemon juice
⅛ teaspoon Tabasco pepper
    sauce

2 cans (8 oz. each) water
    chestnuts, drained
8 bacon slices cut into thirds

In a small bowl combine Lea & Perrins, salt, lemon juice, and Tabasco. Add water chestnuts; cover and refrigerate for 1 hour. Drain. Wrap each water chestnut in bacon; secure with a wooden pick. Arrange on a broiler pan. Place under a preheated hot broiler until bacon is crisp, turning often. Serve hot.

FISH COCKTAIL

about 3 cups

1 cup mayonnaise
⅓ cup catsup
2 tablespoons minced onion
2 tablespoons sweet pickle
    relish

1½ tablespoons lemon juice
1 tablespoon Lea & Perrins
    Worcestershire Sauce
1½ pounds firm-fleshed fish,
    cooked

In a medium bowl combine mayonnaise, catsup, onion, pickle relish, lemon juice, and Lea & Perrins. Flake fish into ½-inch chunks (makes about 3 cups); gently stir into sauce mixture. Cover and chill. Spoon into a serving bowl. Serve with crackers or on small plates with forks.

SHRIMP-STUFFED MUSHROOMS

about 2 dozen

1 pound medium-sized fresh
    mushrooms
1 can (7 oz.) shrimp
1 package (8 oz.) cream
    cheese, softened
¼ cup chopped scallions or
    green onions

¼ cup chopped parsley
1 tablespoon lemon juice
2 teaspoons Lea & Perrins
    Worcestershire Sauce

Remove stems from mushrooms; set caps aside. Drain shrimp, reserving 2 tablespoons of the liquid with the shrimp. In a medium bowl mix cream cheese with scallions, parsley, lemon juice, Lea & Perrins, shrimp, and reserved liquid. Fill each mushroom cap with about 1 measuring tablespoon of the shrimp mixture. Garnish with sliced scallions and parsley, if desired.

CLAM FRITTERS
about 4 dozen

2 cups all-purpose flour	2 eggs, lightly beaten
2 teaspoons baking powder	½ cup milk
1½ teaspoons salt	4 teaspoons Lea & Perrins
1 can (8 oz.) minced clams	Worcestershire Sauce
¼ cup chopped onion	Oil for shallow frying

In a medium bowl combine flour, baking powder, and salt; set aside. Combine undrained clams with onion, eggs, milk, and Lea & Perrins. Stir into flour mixture just until blended. In a large skillet heat about 2 tablespoons oil. Drop batter by the teaspoonful, about 6 at a time, into the hot oil. Fry over moderate heat, until golden, about 2 minutes on each side. Drain on paper towels. Repeat, using more oil, until all of the batter is used.

SMOKED SALMON PINWHEELS *about 16 hors d'oeuvres*

1 package (3 oz.) cream cheese, softened	2 ounces thinly sliced smoked salmon (about 4 slices)
2 tablespoons minced onion	Pumpernickel bread rounds
1½ teaspoons Lea & Perrins Worcestershire Sauce	

In a small bowl blend cream cheese, onion, and Lea & Perrins. Spread about 2 tablespoons of the cheese mixture over each slice of salmon. Roll up, jelly-roll fashion. Refrigerate until firm, about ½ hour. Cut each roll into 4 crosswise slices. Place each slice on a bread round. Garnish with sliced black olives or minced onion, if desired.

HAM 'N' CHEESE ROLL-UPS *about 25 hors d'oeuvres*

1 package (8 oz.) cream cheese, softened	½ teaspoon powdered mustard
1 tablespoon Lea & Perrins Worcestershire Sauce	5 thin slices boiled ham
1 teaspoon chopped chives or parsley	Rye bread rounds

In a small bowl blend cream cheese, Lea & Perrins, chives, and mustard. Spread over ham. Roll up, jelly-roll fashion. Cover and chill at least 2 hours. Cut each roll into ¾-inch slices. Place each slice on a bread round.

STUFFED COCKTAIL MEATBALLS

about 32 hors d'oeuvres

1 pound ground lean beef
½ cup chopped onion, divided
½ cup fine dry bread crumbs
½ teaspoon salt
¼ cup water
1 egg, lightly beaten
2 tablespoons Lea & Perrins
    Worcestershire Sauce

½ cup sliced water chestnuts
2 tablespoons oil
2 tablespoons flour
1 can (10½ oz.) condensed
    beef broth
2 tablespoons dry sherry

In a large bowl lightly combine beef, ¼ cup of the onion, bread crumbs, salt, water, egg, and Lea & Perrins. Divide mixture into about 32 parts; in the center of each stuff a water chestnut slice. Shape into balls. In a large skillet heat oil. Add meatballs, a few at a time. Cook, turning to brown evenly on all sides, about 5 to 8 minutes. Remove meatballs from skillet to a serving dish; keep warm. To drippings in skillet add remaining ¼ cup onion; sauté for 2 minutes. Stir in flour; cook and stir for 1 minute. Gradually blend in broth and sherry; cook and stir until thickened. Pour over meatballs. Serve hot.

10

HICKORY-BARBECUED
CHICKEN WINGS A LA PERRINS   *about 32 hors d'oeuvres*

1 can (8 oz.) tomato sauce
2 tablespoons brown sugar
2 tablespoons Lea & Perrins
    Worcestershire Sauce
2 tablespoons lemon juice
1 tablespoon onion powder
1½ teaspoons cornstarch

1½ teaspoons hickory smoked
    salt
3 pounds chicken wings, cut
    at the joint
Oil
Salt

To prepare barbecue sauce combine in a small saucepan tomato sauce, brown sugar, Lea & Perrins, lemon juice, onion powder, cornstarch, and hickory smoked salt; blend well. Cook and stir until thickened, about 4 to 5 minutes; set aside. Lightly brush chicken wings with oil; sprinkle lightly with salt. Arrange on a rack in a broiler pan. Place under a preheated moderate broiler (350 F.); broil about 10 to 12 minutes, turning once. Brush barbecue sauce over chicken wings; broil until chicken is tender, about 8 to 10 minutes longer, turning and brushing frequently with the sauce. Serve immediately, or freeze in a single layer on a shallow pan, covered with freezer wrap. Just before serving, unwrap and place in a preheated hot oven (400 F.) for 10 minutes, or until hot.

SOUTHERN-FRIED MEATBALLS   *about 5 dozen*

2 tablespoons butter or oil
½ cup chopped onion
1½ pounds ground lean beef
1½ cups cold unseasoned
   mashed potatoes
3 tablespoons Lea & Perrins
   Worcestershire Sauce,
   divided

2 tablespoons chopped parsley
¾ teaspoon salt
½ teaspoon ground nutmeg
Fine dry bread crumbs
2 eggs, lightly beaten
2 teaspoons water
Oil for frying

In a small skillet melt butter. Add onion; sauté until tender, about 5 minutes. In a large bowl combine onion with beef, potatoes, 2 tablespoons of the Lea & Perrins, parsley, salt, and nutmeg. Mix well, but do not overmix. Shape into 1-inch balls. Roll in bread crumbs; set aside. Mix eggs with water and remaining 1 tablespoon Lea & Perrins. Dip meatballs into egg mixture and roll again in bread crumbs. Pour oil to a depth of 1 inch in a large skillet; heat until hot. Add meatballs, a few at a time; fry until golden, about 4 to 5 minutes, turning to brown on all sides. Or, fry a few at a time, in deep oil preheated to 400 F., until golden, about 3 to 4 minutes. Serve hot on cocktail picks. If desired, meatballs may be cooked earlier in the day and reheated in a shallow pan in a preheated hot oven (400 F.) until hot, about 8 minutes.

11

SWEET AND SOUR FRANKS   *about 32 hors d'oeuvres*

½ cup red currant jelly
¼ cup prepared brown mustard
2 tablespoons minced onion
1 tablespoon Lea & Perrins
   Worcestershire Sauce

1 pound frankfurters, cut
   into 1-inch chunks

In a medium saucepan mix jelly, mustard, onion, and Lea & Perrins; bring to boiling point. Add frankfurters; return to boiling point. Reduce heat and simmer, covered, for 15 minutes, stirring occasionally. If desired, serve from a chafing dish with cocktail picks.

SO SIMPLE LONDON BROIL   *12 servings*

2-pound flank steak   Salt to taste
⅓ cup Lea & Perrins   Bread rounds
    Worcestershire Sauce

Score one side of the steak diagonally, 1½ inches apart. Place flat in a tight-fitting glass or enamel pan or doubled plastic bag. Pour Lea & Perrins over meat; cover or seal. Marinate for 5 hours. Remove meat from marinade, reserving marinade. Place meat on a rack in a broiler pan; sprinkle lightly with salt. Broil under a preheated hot broiler, 7 to 8 minutes on each side, basting frequently with reserved marinade. Cut into thin slices on the diagonal. Serve on bread rounds.

CHICKEN LIVERS HONG KONG   *about 2 dozen*
(Low Calorie)

1 pound (about 12)   1 tablespoon dry sherry
    chicken livers   1 tablespoon soy sauce
1 can (8 oz.) water chestnuts,   1 teaspoon garlic powder
    drained and halved   ½ teaspoon salt
2 tablespoons Lea & Perrins   ¼ teaspoon ground ginger
    Worcestershire Sauce

Cut chicken livers in half; place in a medium bowl. Stir in remaining ingredients. Cover and refrigerate for 1 hour. On wooden picks skewer a piece of liver and a water chestnut half. Place on a rack in a broiler pan. Broil under a preheated hot broiler until cooked as desired, about 2 minutes on each side.

CALORIE COUNT: about 58 calories per hors d'oeuvre.

SHERRIED LIVER PATE   *about 2 cups*

2 tablespoons oil   2 tablespoons dry sherry
½ cup coarsely chopped onion   1 teaspoon salt
1 pound chicken livers   ½ cup sweet butter,
2½ tablespoons Lea & Perrins   clarified (see below)
    Worcestershire Sauce

In a large skillet heat oil. Add onion; sauté for 3 minutes. Add chicken livers; sauté until just cooked through, about 8 minutes. Stir in Lea & Perrins, sherry, and salt. Place in the jar of an electric blender; cover and blend until smooth, about 1 minute. Blend in 2 tablespoons of the butter. Pack into small jars or earthenware pots. Pour remaining butter over top to seal. Refrigerate. This keeps well for at least 1 month if kept sealed.

TO CLARIFY BUTTER: Let butter melt slowly over low heat. Pour off clear liquid, discarding milky residue in the bottom of the pan.

CHEDDAR CHEESE STICKS   *about 4 dozen*

1½ cups all-purpose flour
½ teaspoon salt
1 cup (4 oz.) shredded sharp Cheddar cheese

½ cup butter or margarine
3 tablespoons Lea & Perrins Worcestershire Sauce
2 teaspoons cold water

In a mixing bowl combine flour and salt. With a pastry blender or two knives cut in cheese and butter until mixture resembles coarse crumbs. Sprinkle in Lea & Perrins and water. Shape dough into a ball, handling as little as possible. Roll on a lightly floured board to ¼-inch thickness. Cut into strips 3 inches long by ½ inch wide. Place on ungreased cookie sheets. Bake in a preheated very hot oven (450 F.) until golden, about 8 to 10 minutes. Cool on wire racks. Store in a tightly covered container.

CHEESE PUFFERS   *about 20 hors d'ouevres*

5 slices white bread
2 tablespoons butter or margarine, softened
2 egg whites

1 cup (4 oz.) shredded sharp Cheddar cheese
4 teaspoons Lea & Perrins Worcestershire Sauce

Spread bread with butter; cut into 4 triangles. Beat egg whites until stiff but not dry. Fold in cheese and Lea & Perrins. Spoon about one measuring tablespoonful onto each triangle. Place on a cookie sheet. Bake in a preheated very hot oven (450 F.) until puffed and golden, about 5 minutes.

HARDLY COUNTS CHEESE DIP
(Low Calorie)

1¾ cups

¾ cup low-fat cottage cheese
½ cup low-fat plain yogurt
2 tablespoons (1 oz.)
    crumbled blue cheese
2 tablespoons chopped parsley
1 tablespoon chopped scallion
    or green onion

1 tablespoon lemon juice
1 teaspoon Lea & Perrins
    Worcestershire Sauce
⅛ teaspoon salt

In the jar of an electric blender combine all ingredients; blend until smooth. Cover and chill. Use as a dip for fresh vegetables such as celery, green peppers, carrot sticks, or radishes.

CALORIE COUNT: about 19 calories per tablespoon.

14 COVENTRY CHEESE BALL

1 cheese ball

1 package (8 oz.) cream
    cheese, softened
1 cup (4 oz.) shredded sharp
    Cheddar cheese
¼ cup minced onion

2 tablespoons minced parsley
1 teaspoon Lea & Perrins
    Worcestershire Sauce
¼ teaspoon salt

In a bowl blend cream and Cheddar cheeses. Add onion, parsley, Lea & Perrins, and salt; blend well. Shape into a ball. Chill and serve with assorted crackers, if desired.

HARLEQUIN CHEESE BALL: Add 2 tablespoons finely diced pimiento, 1 teaspoon prepared brown mustard, and 1 clove garlic, crushed, to basic cheese mixture. Shape into a ball. Chill. Garnish with pimiento stars, if desired.

HOLIDAY CHEESE BALL: Add 1 tablespoon caraway to basic cheese mixture. Shape into a ball. Chill. Sprinkle ribbons of paprika and chopped parsley around ball.

FRUIT AND NUT CHEESE BALL: Add 1 can (8¼ oz.) crushed pineapple, well-drained, and ⅓ cup finely chopped nuts to basic cheese mixture. Shape into a ball; roll in ⅓ cup finely chopped nuts. Chill.

Opposite: *Coventry Cheese Balls*

WORCESTER CHEESE SPREAD   *about 2¼ cups*

1½ cups shredded sharp
    Cheddar cheese
1 cup mayonnaise
½ cup chopped walnuts
⅓ cup crumbled cooked bacon

⅓ cup chopped parsley
3 tablespoons minced onion
1 tablespoon Lea & Perrins
    Worcestershire Sauce

In a medium bowl thoroughly combine all ingredients. Cover and chill. Spoon into a serving bowl. Garnish with parsley, if desired. Serve with crackers.

MINI CHEESE BALLS   *about 20*

¼ pound sharp Cheddar
    cheese, shredded
¼ cup cream cheese,
    softened

1 teaspoon Lea & Perrins
    Worcestershire Sauce
⅓ cup finely chopped
    pecans

Combine the two cheeses with Lea & Perrins. Form into ¾-inch balls. Roll in pecans. Cover and chill.

16

TWIN CHEESE DIP   *3 cups*

2 cups (1 pint) creamed
    cottage cheese
1 cup (4 oz.) shredded sharp
    Cheddar cheese
⅓ cup chopped onion
⅓ cup dairy sour cream

2 teaspoons Lea & Perrins
    Worcestershire Sauce
1 teaspoon lemon juice
¼ teaspoon salt

In a medium bowl combine all ingredients. Cover and chill. Spoon into a serving bowl. Garnish with parsley, if desired. Serve as a dip for assorted vegetables.

BLUE CHEESE AND CLAM DIP   *about 1⅓ cups*

1 can (10½ oz.) minced clams,
    drained
½ cup dairy sour cream
2 tablespoons blue cheese,
    crumbled

2 teaspoons Lea & Perrins
    Worcestershire Sauce

In a small bowl combine all ingredients. Cover and chill. Spoon into a serving bowl. Serve with chips or vegetable sticks.

CLAM DIP-IT

about 1 ¼ cups

½ cup dairy sour cream
1 can (10½ oz.) minced
   clams, drained
1½ teaspoons Lea & Perrins
   Worcestershire Sauce
⅛ teaspoon Tabasco pepper
   sauce

Combine all ingredients. Chill. Serve with chips or vegetable sticks.

BLACK BEAN DIP

1 ½ cups

1 can (11 oz.) condensed
   black bean soup
¼ cup dairy sour cream
¼ cup minced onion
1 clove garlic, minced
4 teaspoons Lea & Perrins
   Worcestershire Sauce
2 tablespoons chopped parsley

In a medium bowl mash soup. Stir in remaining ingredients except parsley. Cover and chill for 1 hour. Spoon into a serving bowl. Garnish with parsley. Serve with corn chips or crackers.

17

TURKISH VEGETABLE DIP

about 2 ½ cups

1 cup cottage cheese
1 cup plain yogurt
½ cup shredded carrot
½ cup chopped pistachio nuts
⅓ cup minced green pepper
¼ cup thinly sliced green
   onions or scallions
2 teaspoons Lea & Perrins
   Worcestershire Sauce
½ teaspoon salt

In a medium bowl thoroughly combine all ingredients. Cover and chill. Spoon into a serving bowl; sprinkle with paprika, if desired. Serve with assorted raw vegetables.

TASTY DEVILED EGGS

12 hors d'oeuvres

6 hard-cooked eggs
3 tablespoons mayonnaise
1 tablespoon Lea & Perrins
   Worcestershire Sauce
⅛ teaspoon Tabasco pepper
   sauce

Carefully halve eggs. Remove yolks to a small bowl. Reserve whites. Blend mayonnaise, Lea & Perrins, and Tabasco into yolks. Spoon yolk mixture into whites. Chill.

SAVORY SOUPS

Clear or creamy, light or hearty,
soup is everybody's favorite

SHERRIED SEAFOOD BISQUE
8 servings

5 cups water
5 medium-sized potatoes,
   peeled and quartered
½ cup coarsely chopped onion
4 teaspoons Lea & Perrins
   Worcestershire Sauce,
   divided
1 clove garlic, crushed
½ teaspoon thyme leaves,
   crumbled

½ teaspoon salt
1 can (10½ oz.) minced
   clams, undrained
2 cups cooked, flaked fish
1 can (4½ oz.) medium-size
   shrimp, drained
2 tablespoons dry sherry
2 egg yolks
½ cup light cream

In a large saucepan bring water to boiling point. Add potatoes, onion, 2 teaspoons of the Lea & Perrins, garlic, thyme, and salt. Bring to boiling point. Reduce heat and simmer, uncovered, until potatoes are almost soft, about 20 minutes. Stir in clams, fish, shrimp, sherry, and remaining 2 teaspoons Lea & Perrins. Cook until seafood is hot, about 5 minutes. Remove from heat. Combine egg yolks and cream; stir into fish mixture. Heat only until hot. Do not boil. Serve hot or cold. Garnish with paprika, if desired.

Opposite: *Sherried Seafood Bisque*

FISHERMEN'S CHOWDER
about 8 servings

3 tablespoons oil
1 cup chopped onions
½ cup diced carrot
½ cup diced celery
2 tablespoons flour
2 cups water
1 can (1 lb.) tomatoes, broken up

2 packages (12 oz. each) frozen haddock fillets, thawed and cut into 1-inch pieces
1 tablespoon Lea & Perrins Worcestershire Sauce
1 teaspoon salt
¼ cup chopped parsley

In a large saucepan heat oil. Add onions, carrot, and celery; sauté until tender, about 5 minutes. Blend in flour; cook and stir for 2 minutes. Add water and tomatoes; bring to boiling point. Add fish, Lea & Perrins, and salt. Reduce heat and simmer, covered, 15 minutes longer. Stir in parsley. Serve with oyster crackers, if desired.

QUICK 'N' HEARTY CORN AND FISH SOUP
about 4 servings

1 can (1 lb.) stewed tomatoes, broken up
1 bottle (8 fl. oz.) clam juice
1 package (12 oz.) frozen fish fillets, thawed and chunked

1 package (10 oz.) frozen succotash, thawed
1 tablespoon Lea & Perrins Worcestershire Sauce
¼ teaspoon salt

In a medium saucepan combine all ingredients. Simmer, uncovered, until fish flakes when tested with a fork, about 15 minutes.

CREAMED CORN SOUP
about 10 servings

4 slices bacon
¼ cup chopped onion
1 can (1 lb. 1 oz.) cream-style corn
1 can (10¾ oz.) condensed cream of chicken soup
2 cups milk

½ cup water
1 envelope (.19 oz.) chicken-flavored broth mix
1 tablespoon Lea & Perrins Worcestershire Sauce
½ teaspoon salt
¼ cup chopped parsley

In a large saucepan fry bacon until crisp; drain on paper towels; crumble and set aside. In drippings left in saucepan sauté onion for 2 minutes. Stir in corn, soup, milk, water, chicken broth mix, Lea & Perrins, and salt. Bring to boiling point. Reduce heat and simmer, uncovered, 2 minutes longer. Stir in parsley and reserved bacon.

DOUBLE PEA SOUP
8 servings

1 can (1 lb. 4 oz.) chick peas
Water
1 can (11¼ oz.) condensed green pea soup
1 can (10¾ oz.) condensed cream of chicken soup
1 tablespoon Lea & Perrins Worcestershire Sauce
1 teaspoon basil leaves, crumbled
¼ cup chopped parsley

Drain chick peas, reserving liquid and peas separately. To chick pea liquid add sufficient water to measure 2½ cups. In a saucepan combine chick pea liquid and pea soup; mix well. Stir in chicken soup, Lea & Perrins, basil, and reserved chick peas. Bring to boiling point, stirring occasionally. Add parsley and serve hot.

21

HEARTY HAM AND BEAN SOUP
about 10 servings

1 smoked ham shank, about 2 pounds
2½ quarts water
½ cup dried red kidney beans
½ cup dried white kidney beans
½ cup dried pinto beans
¼ cup chopped onion
3 tablespoons Lea & Perrins Worcestershire Sauce
1 bay leaf
2 cups sliced carrots

In a large heavy saucepot combine ham, water, beans, onion, Lea & Perrins, and bay leaf. Bring to boiling point. Reduce heat and simmer, covered, until beans are almost tender, about 2 hours. Stir in carrots. Cover and simmer until beans and vegetables are tender, about 1 hour longer. Remove ham shank; cut off skin from bone; discard. Cut meat into chunks; return to saucepot. Heat until hot.

HOT BORSCHT
(Hearty Beet and Cabbage Soup)

1½ pounds fresh brisket of beef, cut into ½-inch pieces
1 pound beef marrow soup bones
2 quarts water
1 tablespoon salt
1 can (1 lb.) slivered beets
1 can (1 lb.) tomatoes, broken up
3 tablespoons Lea & Perrins Worcestershire Sauce, divided
3 cups shredded cabbage
1 cup shredded carrots
1 cup chopped onions
5 sprigs parsley
2 bay leaves
1 teaspoon sugar
Dairy sour cream

In a large saucepot combine beef, bones, water, and salt. Bring to boiling point. Skim off foam. Reduce heat and simmer, covered, for 1½ hours. Strain beets from liquid; set aside. Into beef broth stir beet liquid, tomatoes, and 2 tablespoons of the Lea & Perrins. Add cabbage, carrots, onions, parsley, bay leaves, and sugar. Bring to boiling point. Reduce heat and simmer, covered, about 20 to 30 minutes longer. Stir in reserved beets and remaining 1 tablespoon Lea & Perrins. Serve with a dollop of sour cream and a sprig of dill, if desired.

22

BLOODY MARY SOUP

2 tablespoons oil
1 cup sliced onions
2 cups diced celery
1 can (1 qt. 14 oz.) tomato juice
4 teaspoons sugar
1 teaspoon salt
1 tablespoon Lea & Perrins Worcestershire Sauce
1 tablespoon lemon juice
⅓ cup vodka

In a medium saucepan heat oil. Add onions and celery; sauté for 3 minutes. Add tomato juice, sugar, salt, Lea & Perrins, and lemon juice. Bring to boiling point. Reduce heat and simmer, uncovered, for 10 minutes. Stir in vodka. Simmer, uncovered, 1 minute longer; strain. Cover and chill. Serve cold.

Opposite: *Hot Borscht*

JELLIED CELERY CONSOMME *2 servings*

1 can (12½ oz.) consommé
¼ cup minced celery

½ teaspoon Lea & Perrins Worcestershire Sauce

Combine all ingredients. Chill. Serve in cups or dessert dishes.

DOUBLE-RICH ONION SOUP *about 8 servings*

2 pounds onions
½ cup butter or margarine
3 cans (10½ oz. each) condensed beef broth
1 soup can water
2 tablespoons dry white wine

1 tablespoon Lea & Perrins Worcestershire Sauce
1 loaf (½ lb.) French bread
¼ cup grated Parmesan cheese
¼ cup grated Swiss cheese
Butter or margarine

Peel and thinly slice onions (makes about 6 cups). In a large saucepot melt butter. Add onions; sauté over low heat, stirring often, until soft and golden, about 30 minutes. Add broth, water, wine, and Lea & Perrins. Bring to boiling point. Reduce heat and simmer, covered, for 30 minutes. Meanwhile, cut bread into 1½-inch-thick slices. Place on a baking sheet; toast in a preheated moderate oven (350 F.) for 20 minutes. Pour soup into an oven-proof casserole or tureen. Place toast on top of soup. Sprinkle with combined Parmesan and Swiss cheeses. Dot with butter. Place in a preheated hot oven (400 F.) until cheese is melted, about 5 to 8 minutes. Serve with additional cheese, if desired.

OLD FASHIONED
VEGETABLE-BEEF SOUP   *about 14 servings*

2 pounds boneless beef
   soup meat
2 pounds beef marrow soup
   bones
2 quarts water
1 can (1 lb.) tomatoes,
   broken up
2 tablespoons salt
2 cups diced turnips
1 small eggplant, diced

1 cup cauliflowerets
1 cup chopped cabbage
2 potatoes, peeled and cubed
2 carrots, sliced
2 zucchini, sliced
1 cup corn kernels
3 tablespoons Lea & Perrins
   Worcestershire Sauce
2 bay leaves
2 tablespoons chopped parsley

In a large saucepot combine meat, bones, and water. Bring to boiling point. Skim off foam. Add tomatoes and salt. Reduce heat and simmer, covered, until meat is tender, about 2 hours. Remove meat and dice; set aside. Discard bones. Add remaining ingredients. Bring to boiling point. Reduce heat and simmer, covered, until vegetables are tender, about 30 to 40 minutes longer. Return meat to soup. Add salt, if needed. Heat until hot.

VEGETABLE SOUP ORIENTAL   *about 6 servings*
(Low Calorie)

5 beef bouillon cubes
5 cups boiling water
2 teaspoons Lea & Perrins
   Worcestershire Sauce
1 teaspoon soy sauce
1 cup thinly sliced carrots

½ cup sliced scallions or
   green onions
2½ cups (½ lb.) sliced
   mushrooms
¼ pound torn spinach

In a medium saucepan combine bouillon cubes, water, Lea & Perrins, and soy sauce. Bring to boiling point, stirring to dissolve bouillon cubes. Add carrots and scallions. Return to boiling point. Reduce heat and simmer, covered, for 10 minutes. Add mushrooms and spinach. Cover and simmer 5 minutes longer.

CALORIE COUNT: about 36 calories per 1 cup serving.

MEAT MAIN DISHES

New ways—some very budget-minded—
with all kinds of meat

MINI MEAT LOAVES HAWAIIAN   *6 servings*

1½ pounds ground lean beef
¾ cup soft bread crumbs
½ cup minced onion
1 can (8 oz.) tomato sauce
1 egg, lightly beaten
4 teaspoons Lea & Perrins
    Worcestershire Sauce,
    divided

1½ teaspoons salt
½ cup drained canned
    crushed pineapple

In a large bowl combine beef with bread crumbs, onion, tomato sauce, egg, 3 teaspoons of the Lea & Perrins, and salt.
Shape into 6 individual meat loaves. Place in a shallow baking
pan. Bake in a preheated moderate oven (350 F.) for 25 minutes. Increase oven temperature to hot (425 F.). Mix pineapple with remaining teaspoon Lea & Perrins. Spoon on top
of each meat loaf. Return to hot oven; bake 15 minutes longer.

Opposite: *Mini Meat Loaves Hawaiian*

PARTY MEATBALLS

4 to 6 servings

⅓ cup chili sauce
⅓ cup beer
1 teaspoon Lea & Perrins
Worcestershire Sauce

1 pound seasoned
browned meatballs

Combine chili sauce, beer, and Lea & Perrins. Heat. Add meatballs and cook for 5 minutes. Serve hot.

ITALIAN STUFFED MEAT LOAF

6 to 8 servings

2 pounds ground lean beef
½ cup soft bread crumbs
1 cup finely chopped onions, divided
1 can (8 oz.) tomato sauce
3 eggs, divided
3 teaspoons Lea & Perrins Worcestershire Sauce, divided
1¾ teaspoons salt, divided
⅛ teaspoon ground black pepper

1 tablespoon butter or margarine
2 tablespoons chopped green pepper
1 cup cooked rice
½ cup chopped tomato
¼ cup shredded sharp Cheddar cheese
1 tablespoon chopped pitted green olives
¼ teaspoon Italian seasoning
⅛ teaspoon garlic powder

In a large bowl combine beef, bread crumbs, ¾ cup of the onions, tomato sauce, 2 of the eggs, 2 teaspoons of the Lea & Perrins, 1¼ teaspoons of the salt, and the black pepper. Mix well, but do not overmix. Place ¾ of the meat mixture into a 9 x 5 x 3-inch loaf pan. Pat gently; make a well running lengthwise in the center of the meat. In a medium skillet melt butter. Add remaining ¼ cup onion and green pepper; sauté until tender, about 5 minutes. Stir in rice. Lightly beat remaining egg; add, together with the remaining 1 teaspoon Lea & Perrins and ½ teaspoon salt and the remaining ingredients; mix well. Spoon rice mixture into the well formed in the meat. Top with remaining meat mixture; pat gently. Bake in a preheated moderate oven (350 F.) until done, about 1½ hours. Let stand in pan for 10 minutes before turning out. Slice and serve.

RITA'S GLAZED MEAT LOAF   6 servings

1½ pounds ground lean beef
1 cup crushed gingersnaps
½ cup chopped onion
¼ cup chopped parsley
¼ cup chopped walnuts
2 eggs, lightly beaten

⅓ cup evaporated milk
2 tablespoons Lea & Perrins
    Worcestershire Sauce
1½ teaspoons salt
¼ teaspoon ground allspice
    Orange Glaze (below)

In a large bowl combine beef with remaining ingredients except Orange Glaze. On a jelly roll or shallow baking pan shape meat into a rectangle, about 9 x 5 inches. Bake in a preheated moderate oven (350 F.) for 45 minutes. Brush Orange Glaze over meat loaf. Bake 15 minutes longer.

ORANGE GLAZE: In a small saucepan combine ⅓ cup orange marmalade, 1 tablespoon lemon juice, 1 teaspoon Lea & Perrins Worcestershire Sauce, and ½ teaspoon ground allspice. Heat gently for 2 minutes.

OUR SECRET STEAK   4 to 6 servings

¼ cup Lea & Perrins
    Worcestershire Sauce
2 tablespoons lemon or
    lime juice
2 tablespoons oil
¼ cup instant minced onion
¾ teaspoon salt
½ teaspoon instant minced
    garlic

3-pound beef loin sirloin steak,
    1½ inches thick
2 tablespoons butter or
    margarine
1 tablespoon chopped parsley
1 teaspoon Lea & Perrins
    Worcestershire Sauce

In a small bowl combine ¼ cup Lea & Perrins with lemon juice, oil, onion, salt, and garlic; mix well and set aside. Place steak in snug-fitting pan. Pour Lea & Perrins mixture over steak. Cover and refrigerate for 2 hours. Remove steak from marinade. Place steak on a rack over hot charcoal. Grill for 7 to 10 minutes on each side, or until done as desired, brushing occasionally with leftover marinade. Remove steak to serving plate. In a small saucepan melt butter. Stir in parsley and 1 teaspoon Lea & Perrins. Pour over steak. Or, if desired, arrange steak on a rack in a broiler pan. Place under a preheated hot broiler; follow preceding directions for cooking.

SAVORY STEAK

6 servings

2 tablespoons Lea & Perrins Worcestershire Sauce
2 tablespoons prepared brown mustard
1 teaspoon lemon juice
1 teaspoon salt
3-pound beef loin sirloin steak, 1½ inches thick

In a small bowl combine Lea & Perrins, mustard, lemon juice, and salt. Place steak on a rack in a broiler pan. Brush with Worcestershire-mustard mixture. Place under a preheated hot broiler for 6 to 8 minutes, brushing occasionally with the sauce. Turn and brush with sauce. Broil until done as desired, about 6 to 8 minutes longer, brushing with sauce occasionally. Or, if desired, place on a rack over hot charcoal; cook following preceding directions.

VERY SPECIAL SPAGHETTI

12 servings

½ pound bacon, diced
2½ pounds ground lean beef
2 cups finely chopped onions
1 cup finely chopped green peppers
3 cloves garlic, minced
3 cans (2 lbs. 3 oz. each) Italian plum tomatoes, broken up
3 cans (6 oz. each) tomato paste
1½ cups water
½ cup Lea & Perrins Worcestershire Sauce
¾ cup chopped parsley
2 tablespoons basil leaves, crumbled
4 teaspoons oregano leaves, crumbled
2 bay leaves, crumbled
4 teaspoons salt
¼ teaspoon Tabasco pepper sauce
Cooked spaghetti

In a large saucepot fry bacon until crisp. Remove and reserve bacon for later use; remove and discard all but 3 tablespoons of the bacon drippings. Add beef; cook until brown, stirring often. Stir in onions, green peppers, and garlic; sauté until tender, about 10 minutes. Stir in tomatoes, tomato paste, water, Lea & Perrins, parsley, basil, oregano, bay leaves, salt, Tabasco, and reserved bacon. Bring to boiling point. Reduce heat and simmer, uncovered, for 3 hours, stirring occasionally. Serve over cooked spaghetti; sprinkle with grated Parmesan cheese, if desired. Freeze any leftover sauce.

WORCESTERED WIMPYS

6 servings

1 tablespoon oil	2 tablespoons Lea & Perrins
1½ pounds ground lean beef	Worcestershire Sauce
1 can (8 oz.) tomato sauce	1½ teaspoons salt
¼ cup chopped onion	6 hamburger buns, split

In a large skillet heat oil. Add beef; cook and stir until brown, about 10 minutes; drain off excess fat. Stir in tomato sauce, onion, Lea & Perrins, and salt. Simmer, covered, for 5 minutes. Serve over hamburger buns.

QUICK BEEF STEW

4 servings

1 can (1½ lb.) beef stew	1½ teaspoons Lea & Perrins
1 can (4 oz.) sliced	Worcestershire Sauce
mushrooms, drained	

Combine all ingredients. Heat and serve.

ENGLISH PICNIC PIE

8 servings

2 pounds ground lean beef	2 teaspoons salt
2 cups soft bread crumbs	2 packages (10 to 11 oz. each)
2 eggs, lightly beaten	pie crust mix
3 tablespoons Lea & Perrins	¼ cup flour
Worcestershire Sauce	3 hard-cooked eggs, sliced
⅔ cup milk	

In a large bowl lightly combine beef, bread crumbs, eggs, Lea & Perrins, milk, and salt; set aside. Prepare both packages of pie crust mix as label directs. Knead for 2 minutes, working in flour. Roll out ⅔ of the pastry to fit into the bottom and sides of a greased 9 x 5 x 3-inch loaf pan, slightly overlapping at the rim. Spoon in half of the reserved meat mixture; top with hard-cooked eggs; cover with remaining meat mixture; pat smooth. Roll out remaining pastry to fit the top of the pan; place on the meat; trim, turn under, and flute edges. Cut out a small circle at the center of the pastry. Using the pastry trimmings, cut out leaves for decoration; moisten bottoms of pieces and gently arrange on pastry. Brush pastry with egg yolk mixed with 1 tablespoon water, if desired. Bake in a preheated moderate oven (350 F.) for 2 hours. Chill thoroughly. Gently run a knife around top edge of the pastry to loosen slightly. Unmold and slice.

ROUND STEAK SIZZLER

8 servings

¾ cup catsup
½ cup Lea & Perrins
    Worcestershire Sauce
⅓ cup oil

1 teaspoon salt
3-pound boneless beef
    round steak

In a small bowl combine catsup, Lea & Perrins, oil, and salt. Place steak in a snug-fitting bowl or doubled plastic bag. Pour catsup mixture over steak. Cover or fasten and refrigerate for 24 hours. Remove steak from marinade. Place on a rack over hot charcoal. Grill until done as desired, about 12 minutes on each side for medium, brushing with marinade occasionally. Or, if desired, place on a rack in a broiler pan. Place under a preheated hot broiler; follow preceding directions for cooking.

ENGLISH PLATE PIE

4 to 6 servings

33

2 tablespoons butter
    or margarine
¾ cup minced onions
1 pound ground lean beef
1 cup chopped mushrooms
2 teaspoons Lea & Perrins
    Worcestershire Sauce
½ teaspoon salt

1 beef bouillon cube
½ cup boiling water
1 tablespoon flour
2 tablespoons cold water
1 package (10 to 11 oz.)
    pie crust mix
1 egg
1 tablespoon milk

In a large skillet melt butter. Add onions; sauté until softened, about 4 minutes. Add beef; cook and stir until brown. Stir in mushrooms, Lea & Perrins, and salt; cook 2 minutes longer, stirring occasionally. Meanwhile, dissolve bouillon cube in boiling water; add to skillet. Blend flour with cold water to make a smooth paste; stir into skillet. Bring to boiling point. Cook and stir for 2 minutes. Remove from heat; cool slightly. Prepare pie crust mix as label directs. Use half to line the bottom of an 8-inch pie pan. Roll remaining half to cover pie. Fill pie shell with beef mixture. Cover with remaining pastry. Trim, turn under and flute edges. Cut slits in top for steam to escape. Brush with egg blended with milk. Bake in a pre-heated hot oven (425 F.) until crust is golden, about 40 to 45 minutes. Cool on wire rack 10 minutes before serving.

Opposite: *Round Steak Sizzler*

SHEPHERD'S PIE A LA WORCESTER   *6 servings*

2 pounds boneless beef for
  stew, cut into 1-inch pieces
⅓ cup flour
2 tablespoons oil
¾ cup chopped onions
½ cup diced celery
1 cup water

2 tablespoons Lea & Perrins
  Worcestershire Sauce
1½ teaspoons salt
1 package (10 oz.) frozen
  peas and carrots, thawed
3 cups seasoned hot mashed
  potatoes

Dredge beef with flour; shake off excess. In a large skillet heat oil. Add beef; brown well on all sides; remove and set aside. Add onions and celery; sauté until tender, about 8 minutes. Return meat to skillet. Stir in water, Lea and Perrins, and salt. Simmer, covered, until meat is tender, about 1 hour. Add peas and carrots; cook, covered, 10 minutes longer. Turn into a 2-quart casserole. Cover with mashed potatoes. Bake in a preheated moderate oven (375 F.) until potatoes are golden, about 20 minutes.

34

THE WORCESTER BURGER   *8 servings*

2 pounds ground lean beef
1 cup soft bread crumbs
½ cup chopped onion
¼ cup Lea & Perrins
  Worcestershire Sauce

1 egg, lightly beaten
1½ teaspoons salt

In a large bowl lightly combine all ingredients. Shape into 8 patties. Place on a rack over hot charcoal. Grill 5 to 8 minutes on each side, basting, if desired, with more Lea & Perrins. Or, if desired, arrange patties on a rack in a broiler pan. Place under a preheated hot broiler; follow preceding directions for cooking.

BARBECUED BURGERS   *4 servings*

1 pound ground lean beef
⅓ cup chili sauce

1 tablespoon Lea & Perrins
  Worcestershire Sauce

Shape ground beef into 4 patties. Combine chili sauce and Lea & Perrins. Brush over burgers and broil.

STEAK ROLL-UPS

6 servings

2 tablespoons oil, divided
½ cup minced carrots
2 tablespoons minced onion
2 tablespoons minced green
   pepper
1½ cups chopped mushrooms
2 tablespoons Lea & Perrins
   Worcestershire Sauce,
   divided

1¼ teaspoons salt, divided
6 individual (2 lbs.) beef
   cubed steaks or chuck top
   blade steaks
3 tablespoons water
1 tablespoon catsup

In a large skillet heat 1 tablespoon of the oil. Add carrots, onion, and green pepper; sauté for 3 minutes. Add mushrooms; sauté for 3 minutes. Stir in 1 tablespoon of the Lea & Perrins and ½ teaspoon of the salt; set aside. Blend remaining 1 tablespoon Lea & Perrins with the remaining ¾ teaspoon salt. Brush ½ teaspoon of this mixture over one side of each steak; turn steaks over. Spoon about 1 tablespoon mushroom mixture on narrow side of each steak. Roll; secure with toothpicks. Repeat. In the same skillet heat remaining 1 tablespoon oil. Add meat rolls; brown well on all sides, about 10 minutes. Remove to serving platter. Add water and catsup to skillet; stir to loosen browned particles from the bottom of the pan. Heat until hot. Spoon over steaks and serve.

35

PANNED BEEF AND BEANS

4 servings

2 tablespoons oil
⅓ cup chopped onion
½ clove garlic, minced
1 pound ground lean beef
1 can (10¾ oz.) condensed
   vegetarian vegetable soup
½ soup can water

1 can (1 lb.) baked beans
   in tomato sauce
1 cup chopped celery
2 tablespoons Lea & Perrins
   Worcestershire Sauce
Cooked macaroni or spaghetti

In a large skillet heat oil. Add onion and garlic; sauté until tender, about 5 minutes. Add beef; cook and stir until browned, about 5 minutes; drain off excess fat. Stir in remaining ingredients. Bring to boiling point. Reduce heat and simmer, covered, until mixture is slightly thickened, about 15 minutes. Serve over macaroni or spaghetti.

MATAMBRE
(Stuffed Steak Chilean)

2 flank steaks (2 lbs. each),
    butterflied
3 tablespoons Lea & Perrins
    Worcestershire Sauce,
    divided
1 clove garlic, minced
1 teaspoon salt
½ teaspoon chili powder

½ pound fresh spinach
2 cups carrot sticks
1 cup onion rings
2 tablespoons oil
2 beef bouillon cubes
1½ cups boiling water
2 tablespoons flour

Open steaks; place long side of one steak over long side of second steak, overlapping by about 2 inches (shingle fashion). Pound the joined ends together to seal. Brush with 1 tablespoon of the Lea & Perrins. Combine garlic, salt, and chili powder; sprinkle over steaks. On steaks place spinach in one layer; arrange carrots lengthwise with the grain; top with onion rings. Carefully roll steaks with the grain, jelly-roll fashion. Tie securely with loops of string. In a large shallow roasting pan place oil. Add the meat roll; brown in a preheated very hot oven (475 F.) for 15 minutes. Remove pan with meat from oven. Reduce oven heat to moderate (350 F.). Spoon off excess fat from pan. Dissolve bouillon cubes in water; stir in remaining 2 tablespoons Lea & Perrins. Pour into pan. Cover securely with heavy-duty foil. Return pan to moderate oven; roast until beef is tender, about 2 hours. Remove meat to a large cutting board; let stand for 20 minutes. Meanwhile, pour pan juices into a large measuring cup; spoon off excess fat. Add additional water or dry red wine, if necessary, to make 2 cups. In a medium saucepan blend flour with pan juices. Cook and stir until mixture boils and thickens. Slice beef roll and serve with gravy.

36

CORNED BEEF FRITTERS

4 servings

1 can (12 oz.) corned beef
1 cup soft bread crumbs
1 tablespoon Lea & Perrins
   Worcestershire Sauce

1 egg, lightly beaten
½ cup milk
1 cup all-purpose flour
1 cup oil

In a medium bowl flake corned beef. Add bread crumbs and Lea & Perrins; mix well. Shape into 4 patties; set aside. In the same bowl combine egg with milk. Gradually stir in flour; beat until smooth. In a medium skillet heat oil. Coat each patty with batter. Fry in hot oil until golden, about 3 to 5 minutes on each side. Drain. Serve hot. If desired, serve with Spanish Sauce (page 120).

GERMAN POT ROAST
(Low Calorie)

12 servings

5-pound bottom round of beef,
   well trimmed
1 cup sliced onions
1 teaspoon minced garlic
1 can (12 oz.) unsweetened
   pineapple juice
½ cup wine vinegar

¼ cup Lea & Perrins
   Worcestershire Sauce
¼ cup water
1 tablespoon salt
1 tablespoon oil
2 bay leaves
Flour

Place meat in a large bowl or a doubled plastic bag. Add onions and garlic; set aside. Combine pineapple juice, vinegar, Lea & Perrins, water, and salt; pour over meat. Cover or fasten; place in refrigerator for at least 24 hours. Remove meat from marinade; wipe dry. In a large heavy saucepot or Dutch oven heat oil. Add meat; brown well on all sides, about 15 minutes. Meanwhile, strain onions and garlic from marinade; add to saucepot; sauté for 5 minutes. Add 2 cups of the marinade and the bay leaves. Bring to boiling point. Reduce heat and simmer, covered, until meat is tender, about 2½ hours. Remove meat from saucepot. Strain gravy; remove excess fat; measure gravy into saucepot. For each cup of gravy blend 1½ tablespoons flour with 2 tablespoons cold water. Add to gravy; cook and stir until thickened. Slice meat; serve with gravy.

CALORIE COUNT: about 280 calories per serving.

POLYNESIAN POT ROAST   *8 servings*

1 can (8½ oz.) pineapple
   tidbits
2 tablespoons brown sugar
½ teaspoon ground ginger
½ cup chopped onion
⅓ cup cider vinegar
3 tablespoons soy sauce
2 tablespoons oil
1 tablespoon Lea & Perrins
   Worcestershire Sauce

5-pound beef chuck arm
   pot roast
1 can (10½ oz.) condensed
   beef broth
1½ teaspoons salt
3 cups peeled sweet potato
   chunks
2 tablespoons cornstarch
2 tablespoons cold water

Combine pineapple, brown sugar, ginger, onion, vinegar, soy sauce, oil, and Lea & Perrins. Place beef in a snug-fitting bowl or doubled plastic bag. Pour pineapple mixture over meat. Cover or fasten. Refrigerate for 12 hours, mixing or turning once. Place beef and the pineapple marinade in a large saucepot or Dutch oven. Add broth and salt. Bring to boiling point. Reduce heat and simmer, covered, for 1½ hours. Add sweet potatoes. Simmer, covered, for ½ hour. Remove beef to a warm platter. Blend cornstarch with water. Stir into liquid in saucepot. Cook and stir until sauce thickens. Serve hot with the pot roast.

HASH-STUFFED PEPPERS   *6 servings*

6 medium-sized green peppers
1 cup water
½ teaspoon salt
2 tablespoons butter or
   margarine
½ cup minced onion
2 cups diced cooked corned
   beef

1 cup diced cooked potatoes
½ cup soft bread crumbs
1 can (8 oz.) tomato sauce
1 tablespoon Lea & Perrins
   Worcestershire Sauce

Cut a thin slice from the stem of each green pepper; scoop out seeds. In a large saucepan bring water and salt to boiling point. Add peppers. Simmer, covered, for 5 minutes; remove peppers, and drain. In a medium saucepan melt butter. Add onion; sauté for 2 minutes. Stir in remaining ingredients. Spoon into pepper shells. Place in a greased 10 x 6 x 1½-inch baking pan. Bake, uncovered, in a preheated moderate oven (350 F.) until hot, about 30 minutes.

Opposite: *Hash-Stuffed Peppers*

OLD-COUNTRY BAKED BRISKET
6 to 8 servings

3½ - to 4-pound beef brisket
¼ cup catsup
2 tablespoons Lea & Perrins Worcestershire Sauce
1 tablespoon lemon juice
2 tablespoons dark brown sugar
¾ teaspoon salt
⅛ teaspoon Tabasco pepper sauce

Place meat in large casserole or baking pan. Place in a preheated very hot oven (450 F.). Brown well, about 25 minutes on each side. Meanwhile, combine remaining ingredients; mix well. Reduce oven heat to moderate (325 F.). Pour Lea & Perrins mixture over meat; cover. Bake until tender, about 3 hours, basting occasionally. Remove meat to a platter or carving board. Skim fat from pan juices. Thinly slice brisket; spoon pan juice over meat. If desired, thicken pan juice with 1 tablespoon cornstarch mixed with 1 tablespoon cold water. Even better if served the next day heated in pan juices in oven or on top of stove.

40

CORNISH PASTIES
6 servings

1 pound ground lean beef
1 cup diced raw potato
⅓ cup chopped onion
1½ teaspoons salt
¼ cup milk
3 tablespoons Lea & Perrins Worcestershire Sauce
2 packages (10 to 11 oz. each) pie crust mix

In a medium bowl combine beef, potato, onion, salt, milk, and Lea & Perrins. Prepare both packages of pie crust mix as label directs; divide mixture into 6 even parts. On a lightly floured board roll 1 part into a 7-inch circle. Spoon about ⅓ cup of the meat mixture into the center of the circle. Lightly moisten the edge with water. Bring opposite sides of the pastry together over the meat; seal and flute with the fingers. Prick top of the pastry with a fork for steam to escape. Brush with milk, if desired. Place on a baking sheet. Repeat rolling and filling 5 more times. Bake in a preheated hot oven (425 F.) for 10 minutes. Reduce heat to slow (325 F.); bake until pastry is golden, about 45 minutes. Serve hot with brown gravy or cold with salad, if desired.

SHERRIED BEEF AND MUSHROOMS

6 servings

2 pounds boneless beef for stew, cut into 1-inch pieces
¾ cup dry sherry
½ cup flour
1 tablespoon dry mustard
2 teaspoons salt
⅛ teaspoon ground black pepper
5 tablespoons oil, divided

2½ cups (½ lb.) sliced mushrooms
1 can (1 lb.) tomatoes, broken up
1 cup diced carrots
1 cup sliced onions
2 tablespoons brown sugar
2 tablespoons Lea & Perrins Worcestershire Sauce

Place meat in a snug-fitting bowl or doubled plastic bag. Add sherry. Cover or fasten; refrigerate for 6 hours. Drain meat thoroughly; set aside. In a plastic or paper bag combine flour, mustard, salt, and pepper. Add meat, a few pieces at a time; coat thoroughly. In a large skillet heat 2 tablespoons of the oil. Add meat, a few pieces at a time; brown well on all sides. Add additional oil as needed. Stir in mushrooms, tomatoes, carrots, onions, brown sugar, and Lea & Perrins. Bring to boiling point. Reduce heat and simmer, covered, until meat is tender, about 1½ hours, stirring occasionally.

SAUCY BEEF AND RICE

6 servings

2 tablespoons oil
½ cup chopped onion
1½ pounds ground lean beef
1 can (1 lb.) tomatoes, broken up
1 can (10¾ oz.) condensed cream of mushroom soup

1 tablespoon Lea & Perrins Worcestershire Sauce
1 teaspoon salt
1 cup packaged precooked rice
1 cup shredded sharp Cheddar cheese
6 toasted English muffin halves

In a large skillet heat oil. Add onion; sauté until tender, about 5 minutes. Add beef; cook and stir until browned, about 10 minutes; drain off excess fat. Blend in tomatoes, soup, Lea & Perrins, and salt. Bring to boiling point; stir in rice. Cover skillet; remove from heat and let stand for 5 minutes. Fluff with a fork. Turn mixture into a 2-quart casserole. Sprinkle with cheese. Bake in a preheated extremely hot oven (500 F.) until cheese is melted, about 5 minutes. Serve over toasted English muffin halves.

DILLED CABBAGE ROLLS

10 to 12 servings

1 head (3 lb.) green cabbage, cored
1 pound ground lean pork
1 pound ground lean beef, divided
1½ cups cooked rice
⅔ cup finely chopped onions, divided
4 tablespoons Lea & Perrins Worcestershire Sauce, divided

1 tablespoon chopped parsley
1¼ teaspoons salt, divided
¼ teaspoon Tabasco pepper sauce
1 can (1 lb.) tomatoes, broken up
1 can (8 oz.) tomato sauce
1 teaspoon dill seed
½ teaspoon sugar

Place cabbage in a large saucepot filled with boiling water. Cover and cook until leaves separate from head, removing them as this occurs. Drain leaves. Trim thick center vein from cabbage leaves, being careful not to tear leaves; set leaves aside. In a mixing bowl combine pork, ½ pound of the beef, rice, ⅓ cup of the onion, 2 tablespoons of the Lea & Perrins, parsley, 1 teaspoon of the salt, and Tabasco. Mix well, but do not overmix. Place a heaping tablespoon of filling in the center of each cabbage leaf. Fold two sides over filling; roll up. Fasten with toothpicks, if needed. In a large saucepot place leftover cabbage. Arrange stuffed cabbage over leaves, seam-side down. In a skillet brown remaining ½ pound ground beef, stirring often. Combine browned meat with tomatoes, tomato sauce, dill, sugar, and remaining ⅓ cup onion, 2 tablespoons Lea & Perrins, and ¼ teaspoon salt; mix well. Pour over stuffed cabbage. Bring to boiling point. Reduce heat and simmer, covered, 2 to 2½ hours.

43

Opposite: *Dilled Cabbage Rolls*

BEEF AND EGGPLANT CASSEROLE   6 servings

1 pound eggplant
3 eggs, divided
½ cup fine dry bread crumbs
1½ teaspoons salt, divided
4 tablespoons oil, divided
⅓ cup chopped onion

1 pound ground lean beef
½ cup diced tomato
2 tablespoons Lea & Perrins
    Worcestershire Sauce
1 tablespoon cornstarch
½ cup milk

Cut eggplant into ¼-inch slices. Lightly beat 1 of the eggs. Combine bread crumbs with ½ teaspoon of the salt. Dip eggplant into the egg, then into the bread crumbs. In a large skillet heat 2 tablespoons of the oil. Sauté eggplant, a few slices at a time, about 1 minute on each side; remove and set aside. Wipe skillet with paper towels. Add remaining 2 tablespoons oil to the skillet. Add onion; sauté until tender, about 5 minutes. Add beef; cook and stir until brown, about 5 minutes. Skim off excess fat. Blend in tomato, Lea & Perrins, and remaining 1 teaspoon salt. Simmer, uncovered, for 5 minutes. In a small saucepan mix cornstarch with milk. Cook and stir until thickened. Lightly beat remaining 2 eggs; slowly stir into the hot milk mixture. Arrange half of the eggplant slices in a 10 x 6 x 1½-inch baking pan. Spoon all of the meat mixture over the eggplant. Arrange remaining eggplant over the meat. Pour egg mixture over all. Bake in a preheated moderate oven (350 F.) for 30 minutes.

44

DEVILED BEEF KABOBS   4 servings

¼ cup Lea & Perrins
    Worcestershire Sauce
2 tablespoons brown sugar
2 tablespoons caraway seed
1 teaspoon onion powder
1 teaspoon salt

½ teaspoon garlic powder
2 tablespoons lemon juice
1½ pounds boneless beef round
    steak, cut into 1-inch
    pieces

Combine all ingredients except beef; mix well. Place beef in a snug-fitting bowl or doubled plastic bag. Pour Lea & Perrins mixture over beef. Cover or fasten. Refrigerate for 4 to 6 hours. Arrange beef on skewers. Place on a rack over hot charcoal. Grill 5 to 10 minutes, turning and brushing with Lea & Perrins mixture 2 or 3 times. Or, if desired, arrange skewers on a rack in a broiler pan. Place under a preheated hot broiler; follow preceding directions for cooking.

BOILED BEEF DINNER

4 servings

2½ pounds beef short ribs
2 quarts water
2 tablespoons Lea & Perrins Worcestershire Sauce
1 cup sliced onions
1 rib celery, quartered
3 sprigs parsley

1 bay leaf
4 teaspoons salt
1 pound carrots, quartered
1 pound small new potatoes
1 small cabbage, cut into 6 to 8 wedges

Cut ribs into individual sections, about 2½ inches wide; trim excess fat. In a large saucepot combine beef, water, Lea & Perrins, onions, celery, parsley, bay leaf, and salt. Bring to boiling point. Reduce heat and simmer, covered, for 1 hour. Add carrots and potatoes. Simmer, covered, for 15 minutes. Add cabbage. Simmer, covered, until beef and vegetables are fork-tender, about 30 minutes. Remove beef and vegetables to a serving platter. Skim excess fat from broth. Serve broth in soup bowls. Serve with French bread, if desired.

45

STEAKHOUSE STEW

6 servings

2 pounds boneless beef for stew, cut into 1½-inch pieces
¼ cup flour
3 tablespoons oil
1 cup coarsely chopped onions
1 can (8 oz.) tomato sauce
¾ cup water

3 tablespoons Lea & Perrins Worcestershire Sauce
2 tablespoons vinegar
2 tablespoons tomato paste
2 tablespoons sugar
½ teaspoon salt
1 can (4 oz.) sliced mushrooms

Dredge beef with flour; shake off excess. In a large heavy saucepot heat oil. Add beef, a few pieces at a time; brown well on all sides. Remove beef; set aside. Add onions to fat remaining in saucepot; sauté until tender, about 5 minutes. Stir in reserved meat along with remaining ingredients except mushrooms. Bring to boiling point, stirring occasionally. Reduce heat and simmer, covered, until meat is tender, about 1½ hours, stirring occasionally. Stir in mushrooms; heat only until hot. Serve over cooked noodles, if desired.

STROGANOFF STEW

6 to 8 servings

3 tablespoons oil
2½ pounds boneless beef for stew, cut into 2-inch pieces
2½ cups (½ lb.) sliced mushrooms
3 tablespoons flour
2½ cups boiling water
¼ cup minced onion

¼ teaspoon minced garlic
1 beef bouillon cube
2 tablespoons Lea & Perrins Worcestershire Sauce, divided
1 teaspoon salt
1 cup dairy sour cream
2 tablespoons tomato paste
2 tablespoons chopped parsley

In a large heavy saucepot or Dutch oven heat oil. Add meat, a few pieces at a time; brown well on all sides. Remove meat; set aside. To saucepot add mushrooms; sauté for 5 minutes. Stir in flour; cook and stir for 2 minutes. Gradually stir in water. Add onion, garlic, bouillon cube, 1 tablespoon of the Lea & Perrins, salt, and reserved meat. Bring to boiling point. Reduce heat and simmer, covered, until meat is tender, about 1½ hours. Combine sour cream, tomato paste, and remaining 1 tablespoon Lea & Perrins; stir into meat. Heat, but do not boil. Stir in parsley. Serve over cooked broad noodles, if desired.

ANDALUSIAN BEEF STEW

8 servings

2 tablespoons oil
1½ pounds boneless beef for stew, cut into 1-inch pieces
2 cups sliced onions
1 clove garlic, minced
1 can (1 lb.) tomatoes, broken up

2 cups water
2 cups sliced white or sweet potatoes, ¼ inch thick
2 cups sliced carrots, ¼ inch thick
1 can (1 lb. 4 oz.) chick peas
1 tablespoon Lea & Perrins Worcestershire Sauce

In a large heavy saucepot heat oil. Add beef, a few pieces at a time; brown well on all sides. Remove beef; set aside. Add onions and garlic to saucepot; sauté for 3 minutes. Return meat to saucepot. Stir in tomatoes and water. Bring to boiling point. Reduce heat and simmer, covered, until meat is almost tender, about 1 hour. Add potatoes and carrots. Simmer, covered, 30 minutes longer. Stir in chick peas and Lea & Perrins. Heat until hot.

Opposite: *Stroganoff Stew*

ALL-AMERICAN "GOULASH"

8 to 10 servings

1 package (12 oz.) medium-
    width egg noodles,
    cooked and drained
1½ cups cottage cheese
1 cup dairy sour cream
4 tablespoons oil, divided
2 pounds ground lean beef
1½ cups chopped onions
1½ cups chopped green peppers

1 can (1 lb.) tomatoes,
    broken up
3 tablespoons Lea & Perrins
    Worcestershire Sauce
2½ teaspoons salt
2 teaspoons Italian seasoning
2 teaspoons sugar
½ cup grated Parmesan
    cheese, divided

Place cooked noodles in a large bowl. Stir in cottage cheese and sour cream; set aside. In a large skillet heat 2 tablespoons of the oil. Add beef, half at a time. Cook and stir until brown. Place beef in a bowl; set aside. In the same skillet heat remaining 2 tablespoons oil. Add onions and green peppers; sauté until tender, about 5 minutes. Stir in tomatoes, Lea & Perrins, salt, Italian seasoning, and sugar. Bring to boiling point. Add reserved meat. Reduce heat and simmer, uncovered, for 5 minutes. Spread half of the noodle mixture in a 14 x 10 x 2-inch casserole. Cover with half of the meat mixture. Repeat. Sprinkle with half of the Parmesan cheese. Bake in a preheated moderate oven (350 F.) until hot, about 30 minutes. Sprinkle with remaining Parmesan cheese; let sit at room temperature for 15 minutes before serving.

48

MEATBALL KABOBS

6 servings

1½ pounds ground lean beef
1 cup fine dry bread crumbs
⅓ cup minced onion
¼ cup sweet pickle relish
¼ cup water
3 tablespoons Lea & Perrins Worcestershire Sauce

1 egg, lightly beaten
1½ teaspoons salt
Green pepper cubes
Cherry tomatoes

In a large bowl lightly combine beef, bread crumbs, onion, relish, water, Lea & Perrins, egg, and salt. Shape into about 18 meatballs. Arrange on skewers alternately with green pepper and cherry tomatoes. Broil over hot charcoal until done as desired, about 8 to 10 minutes, turning occasionally. Or, arrange skewers on a rack in a broiler pan; place under a preheated hot broiler until done as desired, about 8 to 10 minutes, turning occasionally.

49

TANGY SHORT RIB BARBECUE

6 servings

5 pounds beef short ribs
2 tablespoons oil
1 cup chopped onions
1¼ cups catsup
¾ cup water

¼ cup Lea & Perrins Worcestershire Sauce
¼ cup vinegar
2 tablespoons brown sugar
2 teaspoons salt

Cut ribs into individual portions, about 2½ inches wide; trim excess fat. Place on a rack in a foil-lined roasting pan. Bake in a preheated very hot oven (450 F.) until browned, about 20 minutes. Reduce oven temperature to moderate (350 F.). Remove beef and rack from pan; pour off fat. Return beef to pan without rack. In a medium saucepan heat oil. Add onions; sauté for 2 minutes. Stir in remaining ingredients. Bring to boiling point. Reduce heat and simmer, uncovered, for 2 minutes. Pour over beef to coat. Cover and bake in moderate oven until beef is fork-tender, about 2 hours, spooning sauce over beef once. Skim excess fat from sauce in pan. Arrange beef on a platter; serve with pan sauce.

AUSTRIAN PORK WITH RAISINS   *6 servings*

2 pounds lean boneless pork, cut into 1-inch cubes	1 tablespoon Lea & Perrins Worcestershire Sauce
¼ cup flour	1¼ teaspoons salt
2 tablespoons oil	1 tablespoon cornstarch
1 cup orange juice	½ cup water
2 tablespoons lemon juice	½ cup diced orange sections
3 tablespoons dark brown sugar	¼ cup golden raisins

Dredge meat with flour; shake off excess. In a large skillet heat oil. Add meat; brown well on all sides. Remove meat from skillet; set aside. Pour off any oil remaining in skillet. Stir in orange and lemon juices, brown sugar, Lea & Perrins, and salt. Bring to boiling point, stirring to loosen browned particles in the bottom of the skillet. Blend cornstarch with water; stir into skillet mixture. Return meat to skillet. Stir in orange sections and raisins. Simmer, covered, until meat is tender, about 30 to 40 minutes. Serve with hot noodles, sprinkled with poppy seed, if desired.

51

ALSATIAN PORK WITH SAUERKRAUT   *6 servings*

4 teaspoons Lea & Perrins Worcestershire Sauce, divided	2 tablespoons brown sugar
	1 can (1 lb. 11 oz.) sauerkraut, drained
1 teaspoon salt	1 tablespoon caraway seed
4-pound pork shoulder arm picnic	

Combine 3 teaspoons of the Lea & Perrins with salt; brush over pork. Insert meat thermometer into thickest part of the meat, without touching a bone. Place meat on a rack in a shallow roasting pan, fat side up. Roast in a preheated slow oven (325 F.) until meat thermometer registers 170 F., about 2¼ hours. Increase oven temperature to hot (400 F.). Remove pan with pork from oven. Drain fat from pan. Mix brown sugar with remaining 1 teaspoon Lea & Perrins; brush over pork. Combine sauerkraut with caraway seed in roasting pan. Place pork on top of sauerkraut mixture. Roast in hot oven until pork is glazed, about 15 minutes.

Opposite: *Austrian Pork with Raisins*

GERMAN PORK CHOPS   6 servings

2 tablespoons oil	1 can (1 lb.) sauerkraut,
6 pork loin blade chops,	drained
¾ inch thick	1 cup diced peeled tart apple
½ cup chopped onion	1 teaspoon caraway seed
1 beef bouillon cube	1 tablespoon Lea & Perrins
¾ cup boiling water	Worcestershire Sauce

In a large heavy skillet heat oil. Add chops, three at a time; brown well on both sides. Remove and set aside. To skillet add onion; sauté until tender, about 5 minutes. Dissolve bouillon cube in boiling water. Add to skillet along with reserved pork chops. Bring to boiling point. Reduce heat and simmer, covered, until chops are tender, about 40 minutes. Combine remaining ingredients. Spoon over pork chops. Bring to boiling point. Reduce heat and simmer, covered, until hot, about 10 minutes.

PORK CHOPS WITH SAUCE PIQUANT   6 servings

1 tablespoon oil	1 cup coarsely chopped onions
6 pork loin blade chops,	1 clove garlic, minced
½ inch thick	3½ tablespoons flour
2 tablespoons Lea & Perrins	1 can (10½ oz.) condensed
Worcestershire Sauce,	beef broth
divided	½ cup water
½ teaspoon salt	1 tablespoon tomato paste
2 tablespoons butter or	1 tablespoon prepared brown
margarine	mustard

In a large oven-proof pan heat oil in a preheated very hot oven (450 F.) until pan is hot, about 1 minute. Meanwhile, brush chops with 1 tablespoon of the Lea & Perrins and sprinkle with salt. Remove pan from oven. Arrange chops in pan. Return pan to very hot oven; brown chops well on both sides, about 15 minutes. Reduce heat to moderate (350 F.); cover chops and bake until tender, about 40 minutes. In a small saucepan melt butter. Add onions and garlic; sauté until tender, about 5 minutes. Stir in flour. Gradually blend in broth and water. Stir in tomato paste, mustard, and remaining 1 tablespoon Lea & Perrins; mix well. Cook over low heat, covered, for 15 minutes, stirring occasionally. Serve over pork chops.

SCALLOPED PORK CHOPS
AND POTATOES

6 servings

6 pork loin chops, 1 inch thick
3 tablespoons Lea & Perrins
Worcestershire Sauce
½ cup chopped onion

1 package (5.5 oz.) scalloped
potatoes
1½ cups boiling water
½ cup milk

Place pork chops in an 11 x 7 x 1½-inch casserole. Brush Lea & Perrins over both sides of chops. Cover and refrigerate for 30 minutes. Lift up chops; place onion under chops. Place in a preheated very hot oven (475 F.) until chops are browned, about 15 minutes. Reduce oven temperature to hot (400 F.). Arrange potato slices from scalloped potatoes over chops; sprinkle with seasoned sauce mix. Pour water and milk over all. Return to oven; bake, uncovered, until chops are tender and potatoes are golden, about 25 minutes.

PHILIPPINE PORK
AND CHICKEN STEW

8 servings

1 tablespoon oil
1 (2½ to 3 lb.) chicken,
cut into eighths
½ pound boneless lean pork
shoulder, cut into 1-inch
pieces
1 cup chopped onions
1 clove garlic, minced
1 beef bouillon cube
1 cup boiling water

2 cups sliced celery
1 teaspoon salt
2 tablespoons cornstarch
2 tablespoons cold water
½ cup salted peanuts
1 can (5⅓ oz.) evaporated
milk
1½ tablespoons Lea & Perrins
Worcestershire Sauce

In large skillet or Dutch oven heat oil. Add chicken; brown on all sides, about 10 minutes. Remove chicken; set aside. Add pork; brown on all sides, about 5 minutes. Remove pork; set aside. Add onions and garlic; sauté until tender, about 5 minutes. Return chicken and pork to skillet. Dissolve bouillon cube in boiling water. Add to skillet with celery and salt. Bring to boiling point. Reduce heat and simmer, covered, until chicken and pork are tender, about 45 minutes. Blend cornstarch with cold water. Stir in a little of the hot broth. Blend into broth in skillet. Cook and stir until thickened, about 2 minutes. Stir in peanuts, milk, and Lea & Perrins. Heat, but do not boil. Serve over rice, if desired.

HAM WAIKIKI

8 to 10 servings

1 can (1 lb. 4 oz.) pineapple
    slices
1 tablespoon cornstarch
1 tablespoon Lea & Perrins
    Worcestershire Sauce

1 teaspoon ground ginger
3-pound ready-to-eat ham steak

Drain pineapple; set aside slices and juice separately. In a small saucepan combine cornstarch with Lea & Perrins and ginger. Blend in reserved pineapple juice (about 1 cup). Cook and stir over moderate heat until thickened. Place ham on a rack in a broiler pan. Brush pineapple juice mixture over ham. Place under a preheated hot broiler for 10 minutes, brushing once more. Turn ham. Add reserved pineapple slices to broiler rack. Brush ham and pineapple slices with pineapple juice mixture. Broil until ham and pineapple are well glazed, about 10 minutes, brushing once more.

54

OUR EXTREMELY "RAREBIT" (With Ham)

8 servings

¼ cup butter or margarine
⅔ cup all-purpose flour
3 cups milk
1 pound pasteurized process
    cheese spread or mild
    Cheddar cheese, shredded
2 tablespoons Lea & Perrins
    Worcestershire Sauce

⅛ teaspoon Tabasco pepper
    sauce
½ cup flat beer
2 cups diced cooked ham
8 slices toast

In a medium saucepan melt butter. Blend in flour. Stir in milk. Cook and stir over low heat until thickened. Add cheese, Lea & Perrins, and Tabasco. Cook and stir until cheese is melted. Blend in beer and ham. Heat until hot. Serve over toast.

Opposite: *Ham Waikiki*

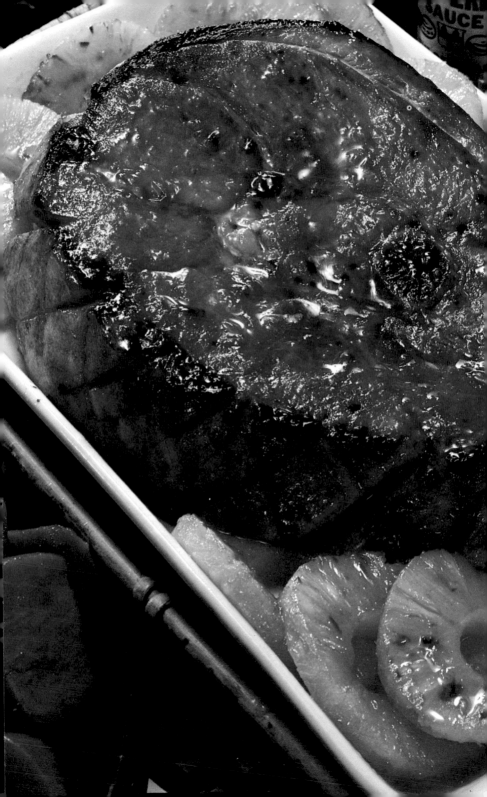

BAKED HAM AND EGG LOAF   *6 servings*

¼ cup butter or margarine,
    softened
8 slices white toast
2 cups diced cooked ham
4 eggs, lightly beaten
3 cups milk

1 cup (4 oz.) shredded sharp
    Cheddar cheese
1 tablespoon Lea & Perrins
    Worcestershire Sauce
¼ teaspoon salt

Spread butter on toast. Cut each slice into fourths. Arrange half of the toast in the bottom of a greased 10 x 6 x 1½-inch baking pan. Top with half of the ham. Repeat layering. In a medium bowl combine eggs, milk, cheese, Lea & Perrins, and salt; mix well. Pour over toast and ham. Place in a larger pan. Pour hot water into the larger pan to a depth of 1 inch. Bake in a preheated slow oven (325 F.) until a knife inserted in the center comes out clean, about 1 hour and 40 minutes.

SKILLET FRANKS IN BEANS   *4 to 6 servings*

56

2 tablespoons butter or oil
¼ cup chopped onion
1 small clove garlic, minced
2 cans (1 lb. each) baked
    beans
1 package (12 oz.) beef frank-
    furters, cut into 1-inch
    pieces

2 tablespoons unsulphured
    molasses
1 tablespoon Lea & Perrins
    Worcestershire Sauce

In a large skillet melt butter. Add onion and garlic; sauté for 2 minutes. Stir in beans, frankfurters, molasses, and Lea & Perrins. Bring to boiling point. Reduce heat and simmer, covered, for 10 minutes, stirring occasionally.

"CREOLE" FRANKS   *6 servings*

1 tablespoon oil
1 pound beef frankfurters,
    cut into ½-inch pieces
1 can (15 oz.) tomato sauce
1 can (12 oz.) vacuum-packed
    corn with red and green
    sweet peppers
1 tablespoon instant minced
    onion

2 teaspoons Lea & Perrins
    Worcestershire Sauce
½ teaspoon marjoram leaves,
    crumbled
¼ teaspoon salt
1 package (8 oz.) elbow
    macaroni

In a large skillet heat oil. Add frankfurters; cook, stirring frequently, until brown, about 5 minutes. Add tomato sauce, corn, onion, Lea & Perrins, marjoram, and salt. Bring to boiling point. Reduce heat and simmer, uncovered, for 10 minutes, stirring occasionally. Meanwhile, cook macaroni as label directs; drain. Serve sauce over macaroni. Sprinkle with grated American cheese, if desired.

CRANBERRY SPARERIBS   *4 servings*

3 pounds pork spareribs, cut into serving-size pieces	1¾ teaspoons salt, divided
	¾ cup jellied cranberry sauce
5 tablespoons Lea & Perrins Worcestershire Sauce, divided	1 tablespoon grated orange peel
	1 tablespoon lemon juice

Brush both sides of the ribs with 4 tablespoons of the Lea & Perrins; sprinkle with 1½ teaspoons of the salt. Place on a rack in a baking pan. Bake in a preheated moderate oven (350 F.) for 1 hour. Pour off fat. Combine remaining 1 tablespoon Lea & Perrins and ¼ teaspoon salt with remaining ingredients; brush over ribs. Continue baking, or place on a rack over hot charcoal and continue to cook until glazed and tender, about 30 minutes, turning and basting both sides of the ribs several times.

57

SWEET AND TANGY   *6 servings*
BARBECUED SPARERIBS

4 pounds pork spareribs, cut into serving-size pieces	2 tablespoons soy sauce
	2 tablespoons catsup
1½ teaspoons salt	2 tablespoons water
¼ cup honey	
2 tablespoons Lea & Perrins Worcestershire Sauce	

Sprinkle both sides of the ribs with salt. Place on a rack in a baking pan. Bake in a preheated very hot oven (450 F.) for 20 minutes, turning once. Reduce oven heat to moderate (350 F.). Cook until almost tender, about 20 minutes longer. To prepare barbecue sauce combine remaining ingredients; blend well. Brush over ribs. Cook 30 minutes longer, brushing and turning frequently.

POULTRY MAIN DISHES

Beautiful birds
with a-little-something-extra flavor

PICNIC FRIED CHICKEN   *4 servings*

2 tablespoons Lea & Perrins
    Worcestershire Sauce
1¼ teaspoons salt, divided
1 (2½ to 3 lb.) chicken,
    cut into eighths

½ cup flour
¼ cup fine dry bread crumbs
Oil for frying

Combine Lea & Perrins with 1 teaspoon of the salt. Brush over chicken. Cover and refrigerate for 1 hour. Mix flour, bread crumbs, and remaining ¼ teaspoon salt. Dredge chicken with flour mixture. In a large skillet add oil to a depth of ¼ inch; heat until hot. Add chicken; fry over moderate heat until chicken is tender and browned, about 25 to 30 minutes, turning occasionally.

COUNTRY CHICKEN   *4 servings*

2 tablespoons oil
1 (2½ to 3 lb.) chicken,
    cut into eighths
1 package (10 oz.) frozen
    mixed vegetables, thawed
1 can (10¾ oz.) condensed
    cream of chicken soup

5 teaspoons Lea & Perrins
    Worcestershire Sauce
½ teaspoon salt
½ cup buttered soft bread
    crumbs

In a large skillet heat oil. Add chicken; brown well on all sides. Remove chicken to a 2-quart casserole. Combine mixed vegetables with soup, Lea & Perrins, and salt; pour over chicken. Cover and bake in a preheated moderate oven (350 F.) until chicken is tender, about 45 minutes. Remove cover. Sprinkle with bread crumbs and bake, uncovered, 15 minutes longer.

WALNUT CHICKEN   *6 servings*

2 cans (10¾ oz. each)   1 tablespoon dry sherry
  condensed chicken broth   2 cups thinly sliced celery
2½ tablespoons cornstarch   2½ cups cubed cooked chicken
1 tablespoon Lea & Perrins   ½ cup coarsely chopped
  Worcestershire Sauce   walnuts

In a large skillet blend broth, cornstarch, Lea & Perrins, and sherry. Add celery. Cook and stir until mixture thickens. Reduce heat and simmer, covered, until celery is just crisp-tender, about 8 to 10 minutes. Add chicken and walnuts. Heat thoroughly. Serve over steamed rice or fried noodles, if desired.

CHICKEN AND LIMA BAKE   *4 to 6 servings*

1 tablespoon oil   6 small onions
1 (2½ to 3 lb.) chicken,   4 carrots, quartered
  cut into eighths   1 tablespoon Lea & Perrins
1 can (10¾ oz.) condensed   Worcestershire Sauce
  cream of celery soup   ½ teaspoon salt
½ soup can milk
1 package (10 oz.) frozen
  lima beans

In a large skillet heat oil. Add chicken; brown well on all sides, about 15 minutes. Arrange chicken in a 2-quart casserole. Drain off excess fat from skillet. Stir soup and milk into skillet. Bring to boiling point; blend well, scraping to loosen browned particles in the bottom of the skillet. Add beans, onions, carrots, Lea & Perrins, and salt. Pour over chicken. Cover. Bake in a preheated moderate oven (375 F.) for 45 minutes. Remove cover. Bake until chicken and vegetables are tender, about 15 minutes longer.

OVEN-BARBECUED CHICKEN AND RICE

4 to 6 servings

1 tablespoon oil
1 (2½ to 3 lb.) chicken, cut into eighths
½ cup chopped onion
1 cup catsup
½ cup water
¼ cup lemon juice

3 tablespoons Lea & Perrins Worcestershire Sauce
2 tablespoons brown sugar
2 tablespoons vinegar
1 teaspoon prepared mustard
½ teaspoon salt
¾ cup uncooked processed rice

In a large skillet heat oil. Add chicken; brown well on all sides, about 15 minutes. Remove chicken to a 10 x 6 x 1½-inch baking pan. Pour off all but 1 tablespoon of fat from the skillet. Add onion; sauté until tender, about 5 minutes. Add remaining ingredients. Bring to boiling point. Pour over chicken. Cover and bake in a preheated moderate oven (350 F.) for 30 minutes. Remove cover. Bake until chicken is tender, about 15 minutes longer.

CHICKEN TIDBITS

6 servings

3 whole chicken breasts, skinned, boned, and halved
⅓ cup flour
1¼ teaspoons salt
2 tablespoons oil
3 tablespoons butter or margarine, divided
2 tablespoons Lea & Perrins Worcestershire Sauce

2½ cups (½ lb.) sliced mushrooms
⅓ cup chopped onion
1½ cups chicken broth or bouillon
2 tablespoons dry sherry
1 tablespoon tomato paste
½ cup toasted sliced almonds

Cut chicken into 1-inch chunks. Dredge with flour mixed with salt; shake off and reserve excess flour (about 1 tablespoon). In a large skillet heat oil and 1 tablespoon of the butter. Add chicken; brown well on all sides. Remove chicken to a bowl. Sprinkle with Lea & Perrins; set aside. Melt remaining 2 tablespoons butter in the same skillet. Add mushrooms and onion; sauté for 3 minutes. Remove to chicken mixture. In the same skillet combine broth, sherry, tomato paste, and reserved flour; blend well, scraping to loosen browned particles in the bottom of the pan. Cook and stir until sauce is thickened, about 2 minutes. Return chicken mixture to skillet. Cover and simmer until chicken is tender, about 15 to 20 minutes. Stir in almonds. Serve in a chafing dish or heated casserole with steamed rice, if desired. This recipe may be doubled if needed.

COMPANY BARBECUED CHICKEN — *8 servings*

1 bottle (5 oz.) Lea & Perrins Worcestershire Sauce
1 cup water
¾ cup lemon juice
½ cup firmly packed light brown sugar
3 tablespoons cornstarch
1½ teaspoons salt
¾ teaspoon ground ginger
6 pounds chicken parts

To prepare barbecue sauce combine all ingredients except chicken in a medium saucepan. Bring to boiling point. Reduce heat; cook and stir until mixture thickens, about 3 minutes. Place chicken on a rack over slow-burning charcoal; grill for 30 minutes, turning often. Brush with barbecue sauce; grill 30 minutes longer, turning and brushing with barbecue sauce often. Or, arrange chicken on a rack in a broiler pan. Place under a preheated moderate broiler (357 F.); follow preceding directions for cooking.

PLUM-SAUCED CHICKEN — *6 to 8 servings*

1 cup damson plum jelly
¼ cup Lea & Perrins Worcestershire Sauce
¼ cup dark corn syrup
2 tablespoons oil
1 tablespoon lemon juice
2½ teaspoons salt
2 teaspoons onion powder
½ teaspoon ground ginger
2 (2½ to 3 lb. each) chickens, cut into eighths

In a large bowl combine all ingredients except chicken; mix until blended. Add chicken pieces, turning to coat. Cover and refrigerate for 1 hour. Place chicken pieces on a rack in a foil-lined shallow roasting pan. Bake in a preheated moderate oven (350 F.) for 45 minutes, basting chicken with plum jelly mixture occasionally and turning once. Increase oven temperature to very hot (450 F.). Bake chicken, basting with sauce twice, until well glazed, about 15 minutes. Remove drippings from pan; skim off fat. Serve hot as a sauce with the chicken.

BARBECUED CHICKEN LEBANESE   *4 servings*

1 (2½ to 3 lb.) chicken, quartered	1 tablespoon lemon juice
3 tablespoons oil	1½ teaspoons salt
¼ cup honey	1 teaspoon onion powder
2 tablespoons Lea & Perrins Worcestershire Sauce	¼ teaspoon garlic powder

Brush chicken with oil. Arrange chicken on a rack over a slow charcoal fire. Grill for 15 minutes, turning occasionally. Meanwhile, combine remaining ingredients; mix well. Baste chicken with honey mixture. Grill until chicken is done, 30 to 40 minutes longer, turning and basting occasionally with honey mixture. Or, if desired, arrange chicken on a rack in a broiler pan. Brush with oil. Place under a preheated moderate broiler (375 F.); follow preceding directions for cooking chicken.

CHICKEN ESPANOL   *6 to 8 servings*

62

3 tablespoons salad or olive oil	2 tablespoons chopped parsley
2 (2½ to 3 lb. each) chickens, cut into serving-size pieces	1 teaspoon salt
1 cup chopped onions	½ teaspoon Italian seasoning
1 clove garlic, crushed	2 cups uncooked processed rice
1 can (1 lb. 12 oz.) tomatoes, broken up	1 package (10 oz.) frozen peas, thawed
1 can (10¾ oz.) condensed chicken broth	1 package (9 oz.) frozen artichoke hearts, thawed
½ cup water	(optional)
3 tablespoons Lea & Perrins Worcestershire Sauce	

In a large skillet heat oil. Add chicken, a few pieces at a time; brown well on all sides. Remove chicken to a 3-quart casserole; set aside. To the same skillet add onions and garlic; sauté until tender, about 5 minutes. Stir in tomatoes, broth, water, Lea & Perrins, parsley, salt, and Italian seasoning. Bring to boiling point, stirring occasionally. Pour over chicken. Stir in rice. Cover tightly. Bake in a preheated moderate oven (350 F.) for 30 minutes. Remove cover; fluff rice with fork. Stir in peas and artichokes. Replace cover and bake 10 minutes longer.

Opposite: *Chicken Español*

CHICKEN BREASTS ITALIENNE   *12 servings*

6 chicken breasts (about 3 lbs.), skinned, boned, and halved
3 tablespoons lemon juice
2¾ teaspoons salt
¼ teaspoon ground white pepper
12 tablespoons butter or margarine, divided
5 cups (1 lb.) sliced mushrooms
½ cup chopped onion
½ cup flour
3 tablespoons olive oil
1 cup water, divided
½ cup dry white wine
1 tablespoon Lea & Perrins Worcestershire Sauce
2 tablespoons chopped parsley

Sprinkle chicken breasts with lemon juice, salt, and white pepper; set aside. In a large skillet melt 6 tablespoons of the butter. Add mushrooms and onion; sauté for 5 minutes. Remove from skillet; set aside. Dredge chicken breasts with flour. To the same skillet add remaining 6 tablespoons butter along with the oil; heat until hot. Add chicken, a few pieces at a time; brown well on both sides, about 10 to 15 minutes. Remove chicken; pour off fat remaining in skillet. Add ¾ cup of the water along with the wine and Lea & Perrins; heat and stir to loosen browned particles in the bottom of the pan. Return chicken and mushroom mixture to skillet. Reduce heat and simmer, covered, until chicken is tender, about 10 to 12 minutes. Remove chicken and mushrooms to a serving platter. Stir remaining ¼ cup water and parsley into liquid in skillet. Bring to boiling point. Pour over chicken and mushrooms. Serve with rice or noodles, if desired.

65

SWEET BARBECUED CHICKEN   *4 servings*

⅔ cup catsup
⅓ cup currant jelly
2 tablespoons Lea & Perrins Worcestershire Sauce
¼ teaspoon Tabasco pepper sauce
1 (2½ to 3 lb.) chicken, quartered

Combine all ingredients except chicken; heat. Brush over chicken and broil chicken until tender, about 45 minutes, turning and basting frequently.

Opposite: *Chicken Breasts Italienne*

CHICKEN NEAPOLITAN
(Low Calorie)

8 servings

2 (2½ to 3 lb. each) chickens,
 cut up and skinned
Water
2 teaspoons salt
2 teaspoons Lea & Perrins
 Worcestershire Sauce
1 clove garlic, minced

1 bay leaf
1 can (8¼ oz.) tomatoes,
 broken up
1 cup diced green pepper
¼ cup chopped parsley
3 tablespoons flour
Celery Noodles (below)

In a large heavy saucepot combine chicken, 1½ cups water, salt, Lea & Perrins, garlic, and bay leaf. Bring to boiling point. Reduce heat and simmer, covered, for 30 minutes. Remove chicken to a large bowl; cool slightly. Remove chicken from bones; cut into chunks; set aside. Skim fat from chicken broth. Pour 1¼ cups chicken broth into saucepot. Add tomatoes, green pepper, parsley, and reserved chicken. Bring to boiling point. Reduce heat and simmer, uncovered, for 15 minutes. Blend flour with 3 tablespoons water. Blend into saucepot. Cook and stir until mixture boils and thickens. Serve with Celery Noodles.

CELERY NOODLES: Remove leaves from 1 stalk celery. Trim and thinly sliver each rib lengthwise; set aside. In a medium saucepan bring 1 cup water to boiling point. Add 1 beef bouillon cube; stir until dissolved. Add reserved celery. Cover and simmer for 10 minutes; drain.

CALORIE COUNT: about 247 calories per serving.

CHICKEN MAGYAR

6 to 8 servings

2 (2½ to 3 lb. each) chickens,
 cut into eighths
½ cup flour
3 teaspoons salt, divided
5 tablespoons butter,
 margarine, or oil
1 cup chopped onions
¼ cup chopped green pepper
1 clove garlic, minced
1 can (1 lb.) tomatoes,
 broken up

2 tablespoons paprika,
 divided
2 tablespoons Lea & Perrins
 Worcestershire Sauce
1½ cups dairy sour cream
2 egg yolks, beaten
1 teaspoon Lea & Perrins
 Worcestershire Sauce

Dredge chicken with flour mixed with 2½ teaspoons of the salt. Shake off excess. In a large heavy saucepan melt butter. Add a few pieces of chicken at a time; brown well on all sides. Remove chicken; set aside. To fat remaining in saucepan add onions, green pepper, and garlic; sauté for 5 minutes. Stir in tomatoes, 1 tablespoon of the paprika, and 2 tablespoons Lea & Perrins. Return chicken to saucepan. Simmer, covered, until chicken is tender, about 30 to 40 minutes. Remove chicken to a heated serving dish; keep warm. Mix sour cream, egg yolks, 1 teaspoon Lea & Perrins, the remaining 1 tablespoon paprika, and ½ teaspoon salt. Stir into saucepan. Heat, but do not boil. Pour over chicken. Serve with potatoes, rice, or noodles, if desired.

SHERRIED CHICKEN-FILLED CREPES *6 servings*

4 tablespoons butter or margarine	2 chicken bouillon cubes
2½ cups (½ lb.) sliced mushrooms	¾ teaspoon salt
⅓ cup finely chopped onion	½ cup dairy sour cream
¼ cup flour	2 tablespoons dry sherry
2 cups milk	2 cups chunked cooked chicken
1½ teaspoons Lea & Perrins Worcestershire Sauce	3 tablespoons finely chopped parsley, divided
	12 crepes (page 113)

In a large skillet melt butter. Add mushrooms and onion; sauté for 5 minutes. Blend in flour; cook and stir for 2 minutes. Add milk, Lea & Perrins, bouillon cubes, and salt. Cook and stir over low heat until mixture is thickened. Stir in sour cream and sherry. Remove 1 cup of the sauce; set aside and keep warm. To remaining sauce add chicken and 2 tablespoons of the parsley. Heat just until hot. Heat crepes, tightly covered, in a preheated moderate oven (350 F.) for 10 minutes. Spoon about ¼ cup of the chicken mixture onto each crepe; roll up. Place two filled crepes on each individual serving dish. Spoon about 2 tablespoons of the reserved hot sauce over each portion. Sprinkle with remaining 1 tablespoon parsley. Serve immediately.

HONEY-GLAZED CHICKEN   *4 to 6 servings*

3 tablespoons lemon juice
4 teaspoons Lea & Perrins
   Worcestershire Sauce
1 teaspoon salt
⅛ teaspoon ground black
   pepper

1 (3 to 4 lb.) roasting
   chicken
1 medium onion, sliced
2 tablespoons butter or
   margarine
¼ cup honey

In a small bowl combine lemon juice, Lea & Perrins, salt, and pepper; mix well. Spoon about 1½ tablespoons of this mixture into the cavity of the chicken; set remainder aside. Place onion into the chicken cavity; close opening. Place on a rack in a roasting pan. Dot chicken with butter. Roast in a preheated moderate oven (350 F.) for 45 minutes. To reserved lemon mixture add honey; blend well. Brush lemon-honey mixture over chicken about every 10 minutes; roast until tender, about 45 minutes longer. Carve and serve with pan drippings.

68

FOLDED STUFFED CHICKEN   *6 servings*

3 (2½ lb. each) chickens,
   halved
Salt
1½ cups soft bread crumbs
½ cup chopped nuts
3 chicken livers, chopped
2 tablespoons chopped
   parsley

3 tablespoons butter or
   margarine, melted
2 teaspoons Lea & Perrins
   Worcestershire Sauce
Lemon Barbecue Sauce
   (page 119)

Sprinkle chicken with salt. Combine remaining ingredients except Lemon Barbecue Sauce. Place a heaping spoonful of this stuffing mixture on the inside of the chicken breast. Break the backbone and fold the leg over the stuffing. Tie the leg and the wing together. Brush with Lemon Barbecue Sauce. Place on a rack over a slow charcoal fire. Grill until chicken is done, about 40 to 50 minutes, turning and basting occasionally with Lemon Barbecue Sauce. Or, if desired, arrange chicken on a rack in a broiler pan. Brush with Lemon Barbecue Sauce. Place under a preheated moderate broiler (375 F.); follow preceding directions for cooking.

GRILLED CHICKEN
WITH APRICOT GLAZE

4 servings

3 tablespoons Lea & Perrins
   Worcestershire Sauce,
   divided
1½ teaspoons salt
1 (2½ to 3 lb.) chicken,
   quartered

1 can (5½ fl. oz.) apricot
   nectar
1 tablespoon cornstarch
⅛ teaspoon ground cinnamon

Combine 2 tablespoons of the Lea & Perrins with the salt; brush over chicken. Arrange on a rack in a broiler pan. Place under a preheated moderate broiler (375 F.). Grill until almost done, about 30 to 40 minutes, turning occasionally. Meanwhile, in a small saucepan combine apricot nectar, cornstarch, cinnamon, and remaining 1 tablespoon Lea & Perrins. Cook and stir until thickened. Brush over chicken; broil until chicken is tender, turning and basting frequently, about 15 minutes longer.

69

LEMON BARBECUED CHICKEN

8 servings

½ cup oil
⅓ cup lemon juice
¼ cup Lea & Perrins
   Worcestershire Sauce
2½ teaspoons salt

2 teaspoons onion powder
1 teaspoon paprika
2 (2½ to 3 lb. each) chickens,
   cut into eighths

In a small bowl mix oil, lemon juice, Lea & Perrins, salt, onion powder, and paprika. Place chicken in a snug-fitting bowl or doubled plastic bag. Pour oil mixture over chicken, turning to coat all sides. Cover or fasten; refrigerate for about 12 hours, turning once. Place chicken on a rack in a broiler pan. Save marinade for later use. Broil under a preheated moderate broiler (375 F.) until chicken is fork-tender and golden, about 1 hour, turning and basting occasionally with marinade. Or, if desired, place on a rack over slow-burning charcoal; follow preceding directions for cooking.

DEVILED CHICKEN

4 servings

½ cup catsup
¼ cup Lea & Perrins
    Worcestershire Sauce
2 tablespoons brown sugar
1 tablespoon prepared brown
    mustard
1 tablespoon water
1 tablespoon oil
1 (2½ to 3 lb.) chicken, cut
    into eighths

In a small bowl combine catsup, Lea & Perrins, brown sugar, mustard, and water; blend well. In a large skillet heat oil. Add chicken; brown well on all sides, about 15 minutes. Remove chicken to a 10 x 6 x 1½-inch baking pan. Pour off fat in skillet. Add catsup mixture; stir to loosen browned particles in the bottom of the pan. Pour over chicken. Cover and bake in a preheated moderate oven (350 F.) for 30 minutes. Remove cover; bake until chicken is tender, about 10 to 15 minutes longer.

70

CHICKEN LIVERS IN RAISIN SAUCE

6 to 8 servings

2½ pounds chicken livers,
    halved
⅔ cup flour
6 tablespoons butter or
    margarine, divided
1 cup chicken broth or
    bouillon
1 cup raisins
1 teaspoon paprika
¾ teaspoon salt
5 teaspoons Lea & Perrins
    Worcestershire Sauce
2 teaspoons lemon juice
1 cup light cream or
    half and half
2 tablespoons chopped parsley

Dry chicken livers on paper towels. Dredge with flour; shake off excess. In a large skillet melt 2 tablespoons of the butter. Add a third of the livers; sear quickly on all sides, about 3 minutes. Remove livers; set aside. Repeat twice more, each time using 2 tablespoons of the butter. Stir broth into the same skillet, scraping to loosen browned particles in the bottom of the pan. Add raisins, paprika, salt, Lea & Perrins, and lemon juice; simmer for 2 minutes, stirring. Gradually stir in cream. Return livers to skillet. Simmer, covered, for 5 minutes, stirring occasionally. Sprinkle with parsley. Serve with noodles, if desired. This recipe may be doubled if needed.

Opposite: *Deviled Chicken*

LIVER AND BACON SAUTE

6 servings

6 slices bacon, cut into
1-inch pieces
1 cup onion rings
1 cup green pepper strips
3 tablespoons flour
¾ teaspoon salt
1½ pounds chicken livers,
halved

2 tablespoons butter or
margarine
¼ cup water
1 tablespoon Lea & Perrins
Worcestershire Sauce

In a large skillet sauté bacon until crisp; drain on paper towels. Crumble; set aside. Pour off all but 2 tablespoons bacon drippings from the skillet. To drippings add onion and green pepper; sauté for 3 minutes. Remove from skillet; set aside. Mix flour with salt. Dredge livers with seasoned flour. In the same skillet melt butter. Add chicken livers; sauté until livers are cooked, about 8 minutes. Stir in water, Lea & Perrins, and reserved onion and green pepper. Heat until hot, stirring constantly. Sprinkle reserved bacon over top. Serve over rice, if desired.

CRISP DUCKLING A L'ORANGE

4 servings

1 (4 to 5 lb.) duckling
3 tablespoons Lea & Perrins
Worcestershire Sauce,
divided
2 teaspoons salt
3 navel oranges, divided
2 tablespoons butter or
margarine

2 tablespoons orange liqueur
1 clove garlic, crushed
2 tablespoons flour
1 can (10¾ oz.) condensed
chicken broth
¼ cup orange juice
2 tablespoons port wine
2 tablespoons sugar

Remove giblets from cavity of duckling; reserve liver for later use. Combine 1 tablespoon of the Lea & Perrins with salt. Brush over cavities and skin. Thinly peel 2 of the oranges. Place peelings inside cavity. Tie legs and tail together. Skewer neck. With a fork prick the skin every ½ inch around the thigh, back, and lower breast. Place on a rack in a roasting pan, breast side up. Roast in a preheated hot oven (425 F.) for 30 minutes. Reduce heat to moderate (375 F.); roast until the legs move freely, about 1½ hours longer. Pour off fat from pan every 30 minutes and prick the skin occasionally.

To prepare orange sauce, grate the peel from the remaining orange (makes about 2 tablespoons); set aside. Cut off the white membrane from the three oranges. Carefully section oranges; set aside. In a medium skillet melt butter. Add reserved liver; sauté until lightly browned. Remove liver; set aside. Into skillet stir orange liqueur; heat 2 minutes. Add reserved grated orange peel, garlic, and 1 tablespoon of the Lea & Perrins; cook and stir 3 minutes longer. Remove from heat and stir in flour. Gradually add broth, orange juice, wine, sugar, and remaining 1 tablespoon Lea & Perrins. Cook and stir until thickened and smooth. Dice reserved liver and add to sauce along with the reserved orange sections. Heat and serve with duckling.

TURKEY WITH FRUITED STUFFING   *4 servings*

12-pound turkey
¾ cup butter or
   margarine, divided
2 packages (8 oz. each) herb
   seasoned stuffing mix
4 cups diced peeled apples

2½ cups orange juice, divided
2 eggs, lightly beaten
3 tablespoons Lea & Perrins
   Worcestershire Sauce,
   divided

Remove turkey giblets; save for soups and stews. To make stuffing melt ½ cup of the butter in a saucepan; stir in stuffing mix, apples, 2 cups of the orange juice, eggs, and 2 tablespoons of the Lea & Perrins; mix well. Spoon into neck and body cavities; secure with skewers. Insert meat thermometer into thickest part of leg, being sure not to touch the bone. Place turkey, breast side up, on a rack in a shallow roasting pan. To prepare basting sauce melt the remaining ¼ cup butter in a small saucepan. Stir in remaining ½ cup orange juice and 1 tablespoon Lea & Perrins; brush over turkey. Roast turkey in a preheated slow oven (325 F.) until meat thermometer registers 180 to 185 F., about 4½ hours, brushing occasionally with the basting sauce. If turkey gets too brown during roasting, cover loosely with a foil tent. Pour drippings into a measuring cup; skim off fat. If desired, thicken drippings with 1 tablespoon flour to every 1 cup drippings. Serve hot with turkey.

TURKEY AND NOODLE BAKE　　　　*6 servings*

2 tablespoons butter or
　margarine
½ cup chopped onion
½ cup chopped celery
1 package (8 oz.) medium-
　width noodles, cooked
　and drained
3 cups diced cooked turkey
　or chicken

½ cup milk
⅓ cup mayonnaise
2 tablespoons Lea & Perrins
　Worcestershire Sauce
½ teaspoon salt
1½ cups (6 oz.) shredded
　sharp Cheddar cheese

In a large saucepan melt butter. Add onion and celery; sauté until tender, about 5 minutes. Add noodles, turkey or chicken, milk, mayonnaise, Lea & Perrins, and salt; mix well. Turn into a buttered 2-quart casserole. Top with cheese. Bake in a preheated hot oven (400 F.) until cheese begins to brown, about 20 minutes.

TURKEY FRICASSEE　　　　*6 servings*

74

2 tablespoons butter or
　margarine
½ cup chopped onion
½ cup finely diced carrot
1 can (10¾ oz.) condensed
　cream of mushroom soup

½ cup milk
3 cups chunked cooked
　turkey or chicken
¼ cup chopped parsley
2 teaspoons Lea & Perrins
　Worcestershire Sauce

In a large skillet melt butter. Add onion and carrot; sauté for 5 minutes (carrots should be just crisp-tender). Stir in soup, milk, turkey or chicken, parsley, and Lea & Perrins. Bring to boiling point, stirring constantly. Reduce heat; cook and stir until hot, about 3 minutes. Serve over steamed rice or broad noodles, if desired.

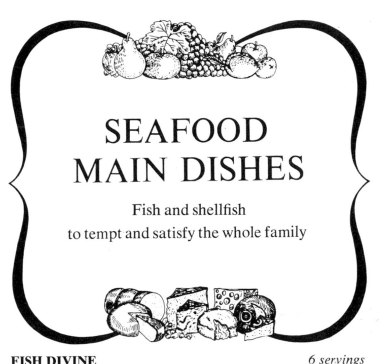

SEAFOOD MAIN DISHES

Fish and shellfish
to tempt and satisfy the whole family

FISH DIVINE

6 servings

1 package (12 oz.) frozen
   fish fillets, thawed
3 tablespoons butter or
   margarine, divided
1 tablespoon lemon juice
½ teaspoon salt
1 package (10 oz.) frozen
   chopped broccoli

3 hard-cooked eggs, halved
3 tablespoons flour
¾ cup milk
1 cup (4 oz.) shredded
   mild Cheddar cheese
1 teaspoon Lea & Perrins
   Worcestershire Sauce

Arrange fish in a single layer in a buttered 10 x 6 x 1½-inch baking pan. Dot with 1 tablespoon of the butter. Sprinkle with lemon juice and salt. Cover with foil. Bake in a preheated slow oven (325 F.) until fish flakes when tested with a fork, about 30 minutes. Meanwhile, cook broccoli as label directs; drain and keep hot. Drain fish stock from baking pan; reserve ¼ cup for later use. Arrange hot broccoli and eggs around fish. Cover with foil to keep warm while preparing sauce. In a small saucepan melt remaining 2 tablespoons butter. Stir in flour. Blend in milk and reserved ¼ cup fish stock. Cook and stir until thickened. Add cheese and Lea & Perrins; cook and stir until cheese melts. Pour over fish, broccoli, and eggs.

FISH COQUILLE

6 servings

1 can (4 oz.) sliced
   mushrooms
Water
¼ cup dry white wine
2 tablespoons minced onion
1 tablespoon Lea & Perrins
   Worcestershire Sauce
⅛ teaspoon salt
1½ pounds fresh or frozen fish
   fillets, cut into chunks
1 package (1 oz.) white
   sauce mix

1¼ cups milk
2 tablespoons grated
   Parmesan cheese
2 tablespoons chopped
   parsley
2 tablespoons diced pimiento
½ cup soft bread crumbs
1 tablespoon butter or
   margarine, melted

Drain mushrooms, reserving liquid; set mushrooms aside. Add sufficient water to mushroom liquid to measure 1 cup. In a medium saucepan combine mushroom liquid, wine, onion, Lea & Perrins, and salt. Bring to boiling point. Add fish. Simmer, uncovered, until fish flakes, about 15 minutes. With a slotted spoon remove fish from the saucepan; set aside. Into liquid in the saucepan stir white sauce mix, milk, and cheese. Cook and stir until thickened. Return fish to sauce. Stir in reserved mushrooms along with the parsley and pimiento. Simmer, uncovered, for 5 minutes, stirring occasionally. Spoon into individual baking shells or casseroles. Combine bread crumbs with butter; sprinkle over fish mixture. Bake in a preheated hot oven (400 F.) until bubbly, about 10 minutes.

FISH STEAKS IN ORANGE SAUCE

6 servings

2 pounds fresh or frozen
   and thawed fish steaks
2 tablespoons orange juice
4 teaspoons Lea & Perrins
   Worcestershire Sauce

1 tablespoon grated orange
   peel
1 teaspoon salt
2 tablespoons butter or
   margarine

Arrange fish steaks in a well-buttered 12 x 7½ x 2-inch baking pan. Combine remaining ingredients except butter; pour over fish. Dot fish with butter. Bake, uncovered, in a preheated moderate oven (350 F.) until fish flakes easily when tested with a fork, about 25 to 30 minutes. Remove fish to a heated serving platter; pour sauce remaining in pan over fish. Garnish with parsley, if desired.

IMPERIAL FISH BALTIMORE

4 servings

3 tablespoons butter or
  margarine, divided
½ cup diced green pepper
¼ cup mayonnaise
2 teaspoons Lea & Perrins
  Worcestershire Sauce
¼ teaspoon salt
¼ teaspoon powdered mustard
2 cups flaked cooked white
  fish
¾ cup soft bread crumbs
¼ cup chopped pimiento
½ teaspoon paprika

In a medium saucepan melt 1 tablespoon of the butter. Add green pepper; sauté for 2 minutes. Remove from heat; stir in mayonnaise, Lea & Perrins, salt, and mustard. Gently blend in fish. Turn into a buttered 1-quart casserole. In a small saucepan melt remaining 2 tablespoons butter. Stir in bread crumbs, pimiento, and paprika. Sprinkle over fish mixture. Bake in a preheated moderate oven (350 F.) until crumbs are golden, about 30 minutes.

77

PORTUGUESE FISH

4 servings

2 tablespoons olive oil
½ cup chopped onion
1 clove garlic, minced
1 can (8¼ oz.) tomatoes,
  broken up
3 tablespoons tomato paste
2 teaspoons Lea & Perrins
  Worcestershire Sauce
1½ teaspoons salt
1 teaspoon sugar
1½ cups cooked rice
1 package (1 lb.) frozen
  fillet of flounder,
  thawed

In a medium saucepan heat oil. Add onion and garlic; sauté for 2 minutes. Stir in tomatoes, tomato paste, Lea & Perrins, salt, and sugar. Bring to boiling point. Reduce heat and simmer, uncovered, for 5 minutes. Stir in rice; heat until hot. Arrange half of the rice mixture in a buttered 10 x 6 x 1½-inch baking pan. Top with fish fillets, then remaining rice. Bake, uncovered, in a preheated moderate oven (350 F.) until fish flakes easily when tested with a fork, about 20 minutes.

SHRIMP-STUFFED FISH FILLETS
6 to 8 servings

3 tablespoons butter or
   margarine
½ cup minced celery
3 tablespoons minced onion
1 can (4½ oz.) medium
   shrimp, divided
1½ cups soft bread crumbs
1 egg, lightly beaten
4 teaspoons Lea & Perrins
   Worcestershire Sauce,
   divided

6 to 8 (2 lbs.) fillets of sole or
   flounder
1 can (10¾ oz.) condensed
   cream of shrimp soup
¼ cup milk
1 tablespoon chopped
   parsley

In a small skillet melt butter. Add celery and onion; sauté until tender, about 5 minutes. Drain and rinse shrimp, reserving ¼ cup shrimp for sauce. Finely chop remaining shrimp. In a small bowl combine shrimp with celery and onion. Stir in bread crumbs, egg, and 3 teaspoons of the Lea & Perrins; mix well. Place a heaping tablespoon of stuffing on each fillet. Roll tightly. Fasten with a toothpick if necessary. Place in an 11 x 7½ x 2-inch baking pan; set aside. In a small saucepan combine soup, milk, and parsley with reserved ¼ cup shrimp and remaining 1 teaspoon Lea & Perrins; mix well. Heat only until hot. Pour over fish rolls. Cover and bake in a preheated moderate oven (350 F.) until fish flakes easily when tested with a fork, about 40 minutes.

78

SAVORY FISH SALAD
6 servings

2 packages (12 oz. each)
   frozen fish fillets, thawed
1 cup diced celery
¼ cup chopped onion
2 tablespoons diced pimiento

¼ cup oil
1 tablespoon lemon juice
1½ teaspoons Lea & Perrins
   Worcestershire Sauce
½ teaspoon salt

In a medium skillet bring 1 inch of water to boiling point. Add fish; poach for 6 to 8 minutes. With a slotted spoon remove fish from the water to a mixing bowl. Cool and flake. Chill thoroughly. Add celery, onion, and pimiento. Mix oil with lemon juice, Lea & Perrins, and salt. Pour over fish mixture. Toss well. Serve on lettuce leaves garnished with tomato wedges and radish roses, if desired.

Opposite: *Shrimp-Stuffed Fish Fillets*

HALIBUT STEAKS A LA PERRINS   *8 servings*

¼ cup butter or margarine
2 tablespoons Lea & Perrins
   Worcestershire Sauce
4 teaspoons lemon juice

1½ teaspoons salt
4 pounds halibut steaks
1½ cups soft bread crumbs

In a small saucepan melt butter. Stir in Lea & Perrins, lemon juice, and salt. Lightly brush halibut steaks on both sides with about half of the butter mixture; place on a buttered jelly roll pan. Bake, uncovered, in a preheated moderate (350 F.) oven until fish flakes easily when tested with a fork, about 20 minutes. Remove fish from oven. Increase oven temperature to very hot (450 F.). Stir bread crumbs into remaining butter mixture in saucepan. Spoon over halibut steaks. Return fish to very hot oven; bake until crumbs are golden, about 7 minutes.

FISH STICKS ORLEANS   *6 servings*

2 packages (9 oz. each) frozen
   fish sticks with sauce mix
2 tablespoons butter or
   margarine
2 tablespoons minced onion
1 can (1 lb.) tomatoes,
   broken up

½ cup diced green pepper
2 teaspoons Lea & Perrins
   Worcestershire Sauce
½ teaspoon salt

Prepare fish sticks as label directs. Reserve packets of sauce mix. Meanwhile, in a medium saucepan melt butter. Add onion; sauté until tender, about 5 minutes. Stir in tomatoes, green pepper, Lea & Perrins, and salt. Bring to boiling point. Reduce heat and simmer, uncovered, until sauce is slightly thickened, about 10 minutes. Stir in reserved sauce mix. Serve over hot fish sticks.

SALMON-FILLED CREPES   *6 servings*

6 tablespoons butter or
   margarine
2½ cups (½ lb.) sliced
   mushrooms
1 cup diced celery
⅓ cup chopped onion
⅓ cup all-purpose flour
2 chicken bouillon cubes
1½ cups boiling water

1 teaspoon Lea & Perrins
   Worcestershire Sauce
1 teaspoon lemon juice
1 can (1 lb.) salmon,
   drained and flaked
1 cup dairy sour cream
2 tablespoons chopped parsley
12 crepes (page 113)
1 cup shredded Swiss cheese

In a large skillet melt butter. Add mushrooms; sauté for 2 minutes. Add celery and onion; sauté for 3 minutes. Blend in flour; cook and stir over low heat for 1 minute. Dissolve bouillon cubes in boiling water. Add to mushroom mixture with Lea & Perrins and lemon juice. Cook and stir over low heat until mixture is thickened, about 2 minutes. Blend in salmon, sour cream, and parsley. Heat just until hot. Place about ¼ cup of this mixture on each crepe; roll up and place seam side down in a buttered 12 x 7½ x 2-inch baking pan. Spoon remaining filling over crepes. Sprinkle cheese over all. Bake in a preheated moderate oven (350 F.) for 20 minutes, or until hot and cheese is melted. If desired, place under a preheated hot broiler for 2 minutes to brown cheese. Serve with lemon wedges, if desired.

SALMON SUPPER   *8 servings*

1 pound elbow macaroni, cooked and drained
1 can (1 lb.) salmon, drained and chunked
1 small tomato, diced
2 cans (11 oz. each) condensed Cheddar cheese soup
1½ cups milk
2 tablespoons minced onion
4 teaspoons Lea & Perrins Worcestershire Sauce
⅛ teaspoon ground red pepper
½ cup soft bread crumbs
1 tablespoon butter or margarine, melted

Place cooked macaroni in a 3-quart casserole. Top with salmon and tomato. In a medium saucepan combine soup with milk. Stir in onion, Lea & Perrins, and red pepper. Heat, but do not boil. Pour soup mixture over all. Combine bread crumbs with butter; sprinkle over macaroni mixture. Bake, uncovered, in a preheated moderate oven (375 F.) for 30 minutes. Garnish with sliced tomatoes, if desired.

SCAMPI   *2 to 3 servings*

⅓ cup Lea & Perrins Worcestershire Sauce
2 tablespoons oil
2 tablespoons lemon juice
½ teaspoon garlic powder
⅛ teaspoon Tabasco pepper sauce
½ pound peeled and deveined raw shrimp

Combine all ingredients except shrimp. Pour marinade over shrimp and broil about 3 minutes, basting occasionally. Serve with rice if desired.

BEANS AND RICE

Hearty and flavorful,
some of these are meals in themselves

MUSHROOM-RICE RING AMANDINE   8 servings

¼ cup butter or margarine
2½ cups (½ lb.) sliced mushrooms
¾ cup chopped onions
1¾ cups uncooked processed rice
1 can (10¾ oz.) condensed chicken broth
2¾ cups water
1 tablespoon Lea & Perrins Worcestershire Sauce
½ teaspoon salt
⅓ cup toasted sliced almonds
¼ cup chopped parsley
2 packages (10 oz. each) frozen green peas, cooked and drained

In a large skillet melt butter. Add mushrooms and onions; sauté until tender, about 5 minutes. Stir in rice, broth, water, Lea & Perrins, and salt. Bring to boiling point. Reduce heat and simmer, covered, until rice is tender and liquid is absorbed, about 25 minutes. Stir in almonds and parsley. Pack into a buttered 6-cup ring mold. Unmold onto a heated platter. Fill center of ring with hot peas.

Opposite: *Mushroom-Rice Ring Amandine*

OUR BEST FRIED RICE   *4 servings*

4 slices bacon
1 cup diced green pepper
½ cup chopped onion
2 cups cooked rice

2 teaspoons Lea & Perrins
   Worcestershire Sauce
¼ teaspoon salt

In a medium skillet cook bacon until crisp; drain on paper towels; crumble and set aside. Pour off all but 2 tablespoons of the bacon drippings. To drippings in skillet add green pepper and onion; sauté for 3 minutes. Add rice; stir-fry until golden brown, about 5 minutes. Stir in Lea & Perrins, salt, and reserved bacon; heat until hot.

"CELERIED" RICE   *6 servings*

1 can (10¾ oz.) condensed
   cream of celery soup
1 cup water
2 tablespoons instant minced
   onion

1 teaspoon Lea & Perrins
   Worcestershire Sauce
2 cups packaged precooked rice
2 tablespoons parsley flakes

In a medium saucepan bring soup, water, onion, and Lea & Perrins to boiling point. Stir in rice and parsley flakes. Turn off heat. Cover and let sit for 5 minutes. Fluff with a fork before serving.

ARABIAN RICE   *8 servings*

¼ cup butter or margarine
2 cups uncooked processed
   rice
¼ cup pine nuts
2 cans (10½ oz. each)
   condensed beef broth
2½ cups water

¼ cup raisins
2 teaspoons Lea & Perrins
   Worcestershire Sauce
½ teaspoon ground allspice
½ teaspoon ground nutmeg
½ teaspoon ground cinnamon

In a large skillet melt butter. Add rice and pine nuts. Fry, stirring constantly, until rice and nuts are golden, about 5 minutes. Stir in remaining ingredients. Bring to boiling point. Reduce heat and simmer, covered, until rice is tender and liquid is absorbed, about 25 minutes.

CASSOULET

8 to 10 servings

1 pound dried Great
    Northern beans
1½ quarts water
¼ pound salt pork
1 cup sliced onions
2 teaspoons salt
1 bay leaf
4 whole cloves
4 tablespoons Lea & Perrins
    Worcestershire Sauce,
    divided

2 tablespoons oil
2½ pounds boneless lean pork,
    cut into 1-inch pieces
1 can (1 lb.) tomatoes,
    broken up
½ cup dry white wine
½ pound Polish sausage links,
    cut into 1-inch pieces
2 cups sliced carrots
2 cups diced cooked chicken
    or turkey

Wash beans; drain. In a large heavy saucepot combine beans, water, salt pork, onions, salt, bay leaf, cloves, and 2 tablespoons of the Lea & Perrins. Bring to boiling point. Reduce heat and simmer, covered, for 1½ hours. In a large skillet heat oil. Add half of the pork at a time; brown well on both sides. Add pork to bean mixture. Into skillet stir tomatoes, wine, and remaining 2 tablespoons Lea & Perrins, scraping to loosen browned particles in the bottom of the pan. Pour into bean mixture along with sausage and carrots; mix well. Bring to boiling point. Reduce heat and simmer, covered, until meat and beans are tender, about 2 hours, stirring occasionally and adding boiling water if necessary to cover beans. Stir in chicken. Heat until hot.

SASSY BEAN BAKE

6 servings

8 slices bacon, cut into
    1-inch pieces
1 can (8 oz.) tomato sauce
¼ cup firmly packed dark
    brown sugar
2 tablespoons Lea & Perrins
    Worcestershire Sauce

1½ teaspoons prepared brown
    mustard
½ teaspoon salt
3 cans (1 lb. each) baked
    beans with pork in
    tomato sauce
1 cup chopped onions

In a small skillet fry bacon until almost crisp; drain on paper towels; set aside. In a mixing bowl combine tomato sauce, brown sugar, Lea & Perrins, mustard, and salt; blend well. Add beans, onions, and reserved bacon; blend well. Turn into a 2-quart casserole or bean pot. Bake, uncovered, in a preheated slow oven (300 F.) until flavors mingle, about 1 hour.

KIDNEY BEAN CASSEROLE 6 to 8 servings

1 cup dried red kidney beans
1 cup dried white kidney
   beans
About 6 cups water
2 cups diced peeled tart apples
½ cup chopped onion
3 tablespoons brown sugar
3 tablespoons Lea & Perrins
   Worcestershire Sauce
3 tablespoons unsulphured
   molasses
2 teaspoons salt
½ pound salt pork

Wash beans; drain. Place in a large heavy saucepan. Add water. Bring to boiling point. Reduce heat and simmer, covered, until skins pop, about 40 minutes. Drain beans, reserving liquid. Place beans in a 2-quart bean pot or casserole. Combine 2 cups of the reserved bean liquid (add water to make 2 cups if necessary) with the apples, onion, sugar, Lea & Perrins, molasses, and salt; stir into beans. Score salt pork, making cuts ½ inch apart and 1 inch deep. Bury in the center of the beans. Cover the bean pot. Bake in a preheated slow oven (325 F.) until beans are tender, about 5 hours, stirring once or twice, adding boiling water if necessary to cover beans.

86

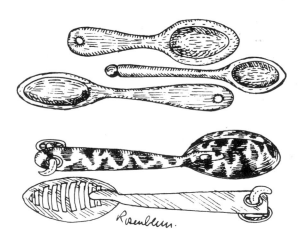

Opposite: *Kidney Bean Casserole*

EGGS AND CHEESE

Good, low-budget ways
to assure the family of ample protein

HUEVOS RANCHEROS
6 servings

4 tablespoons oil, divided
¼ cup minced onion
1 can (1 lb.) tomatoes,
    broken up
2 teaspoons Lea & Perrins
    Worcestershire Sauce
½ teaspoon salt
½ teaspoon sugar

½ teaspoon chili powder
12 tortillas
6 tablespoons butter or
    margarine, divided
12 eggs, divided
1 ripe avocado, peeled,
    pitted, and chunked

In a medium saucepan heat 1 tablespoon of the oil. Add onion; sauté for 1 minute. Add tomatoes, Lea & Perrins, salt, sugar, and chili powder. Bring to boiling point. Reduce heat and simmer, uncovered, for 15 minutes. In a large skillet heat remaining 3 tablespoons oil. Add tortillas, 3 at a time; fry lightly, about 1 minute. Drain tortillas on paper towels; keep hot. In the same skillet melt 2 tablespoons of the butter. Crack 4 eggs into the skillet; fry lightly. Repeat, using remaining butter and eggs. Place an egg on each tortilla. For each serving spoon tomato sauce on an individual serving plate; place 2 egg-topped tortillas over sauce. Garnish with avocado chunks.

Opposite: *Huevos Rancheros*

CHEDDAR SOUFFLE

6 servings

¼ cup butter or margarine
¼ cup all-purpose flour
1½ cups milk
3 cups (12 oz.) shredded
sharp Cheddar cheese

1 teaspoon salt
6 eggs, separated
2 tablespoons Lea & Perrins
Worcestershire Sauce

In the top portion of a double boiler melt butter. Blend in flour. Stir in milk. Cook and stir until thickened. Add cheese and salt. Place over hot water; cook and stir until cheese melts. Remove from heat. In a large bowl beat egg yolks. Gradually stir in cheese sauce; beat until well blended. Stir in Lea & Perrins. Beat egg whites until soft peaks form. Gently fold into cheese mixture. Turn into a 2-quart straight-sided soufflé dish with only the bottom buttered. Place in a larger pan. Pour hot water into the larger pan to a depth of 2 inches. Bake in a preheated slow oven (325 F.) until soufflé is firm, about 1 hour and 10 minutes. If soufflé is browning too fast, cover lightly with a sheet of aluminum foil. This soufflé holds well for 10 minutes after removing from oven.

"SOUPER" CHEESE AND CELERY SOUFFLE

4 servings

1 can (10¾ oz.) condensed cream of celery soup
1 cup (4 oz.) shredded sharp Cheddar cheese
2 tablespoons minced onion
2 tablespoons minced celery
2 teaspoons Lea & Perrins Worcestershire Sauce
2 tablespoons finely chopped celery leaves
6 eggs, separated
½ teaspoon cream of tartar

Make a 4-inch wide band of triple thickness aluminum foil 2 inches longer than the circumference of a 2-quart soufflé dish. Wrap band around top of the dish so that height of the dish is raised. Butter the inside of the dish and the foil; set aside. In a small saucepan combine soup, cheese, onion, and celery. Cook and stir over low heat until cheese is melted. Remove from heat; stir in Lea & Perrins and celery leaves; set aside. In a large mixing bowl beat egg whites and cream of tartar until stiff but not dry. In a small mixing bowl beat egg yolks until thick and light in color. Stir yolks into cheese mixture. Stir one fourth of the egg whites into cheese mixture, then fold remaining egg whites into cheese mixture. Pour into the prepared soufflé dish. Bake in a preheated moderate oven (350 F.) until a knife inserted into the center comes out clean, about 50 to 60 minutes. Carefully remove foil from dish. Serve soufflé immediately.

COTTAGE CHEESE AND SPINACH SCRAMBLE

6 servings

6 eggs, lightly beaten
1 cup creamed cottage cheese
¼ cup milk
1 teaspoon salt
1 teaspoon onion powder
1 tablespoon Lea & Perrins Worcestershire Sauce
2 tablespoons butter or margarine
1 package (10 oz.) frozen chopped spinach, thawed

Combine eggs, cottage cheese, milk, salt, onion powder, and Lea & Perrins. In a large skillet melt butter. Add egg mixture. Cook over low heat, stirring gently, until eggs are almost set. Add spinach. Cook and stir until eggs are done as desired and spinach is hot, about 2 minutes.

SCOTCH EGGS

6 eggs

6 hard-cooked eggs
2 tablespoons flour
1 pound bulk sausage meat
1½ tablespoons Lea & Perrins
Worcestershire Sauce

1 egg, lightly beaten
¾ cup fine dry bread crumbs
¼ cup salad oil
Herbed Tomato Sauce (below)

Peel eggs; dust with flour. Mix sausage meat with Lea & Perrins; divide into 6 equal parts. Flatten each portion into a thin oval patty and mold evenly around one egg, making sure there are no cracks in the sausage meat. Dip into beaten egg, then roll in bread crumbs, gently patting bread crumbs into place. Repeat with each egg. In a large skillet heat oil. Add eggs, 3 at a time; sauté until sausage is cooked, about 7 minutes, turning occasionally. Or, if desired, fry eggs, 3 at a time, in deep fat preheated to 325 F., until sausage is cooked, about 7 minutes. Drain on paper towels. Serve immediately with Herbed Tomato Sauce or cool and serve in halves as an hors d'oeuvre.

Herbed Tomato Sauce

2 cups

4 slices bacon, diced
½ cup minced onion
2 tablespoons flour
1 can (1 lb.) tomatoes,
broken up

1 tablespoon Lea & Perrins
Worcestershire Sauce
¼ teaspoon rosemary leaves,
crumbled

In a medium saucepan lightly fry bacon. Add onion; sauté for 3 minutes. Add flour; cook and stir for 1 minute. Blend in tomatoes, Lea & Perrins, and rosemary. Bring to boiling point. Reduce heat and simmer, covered, for 10 minutes. Serve as is, or push through a strainer or puree in an electric blender; reheat. Serve over hot Scotch Eggs.

SPINACH OMELET

4 servings

2 tablespoons butter or
    margarine, divided
2 tablespoons minced onion
½ teaspoon minced garlic
1 package (10 oz.) frozen
    chopped spinach, cooked
    and drained
1 tablespoon diced pimiento
1 tablespoon chopped parsley
2½ teaspoons Lea & Perrins
    Worcestershire Sauce,
    divided

¾ teaspoon salt, divided
¼ teaspoon basil leaves,
    crumbled
6 eggs
2 tablespoons light cream
2 tablespoons grated
    Parmesan cheese, divided
1 tablespoon olive oil

In a small skillet melt 1 tablespoon of the butter. Add onion and garlic; sauté for 3 to 4 minutes. Add spinach, pimiento, parsley, 1½ teaspoons of the Lea & Perrins, ¼ teaspoon of the salt, and basil; blend; set aside. In a bowl combine eggs, cream, 1 tablespoon of the Parmesan cheese, the remaining 1 teaspoon Lea & Perrins, and ½ teaspoon salt; blend with wire whip. In a 10-inch skillet melt remaining 1 tablespoon butter and the oil. Pour in egg mixture. Cook over low heat until mixture is still moist on the top. Remove from heat. Scatter spinach mixture over egg. Sprinkle with remaining 1 tablespoon Parmesan cheese. Place in a preheated very hot oven (450 F.) until egg is set, about 4 to 5 minutes. Slice into wedges and serve.

93

CHEDDAR'D BEANS

4 to 6 servings

2 tablespoons butter or
    margarine
1 cup chopped onions
1 can (1 lb.) kidney beans,
    drained and crushed
2 cups (8 oz.) shredded
    mild Cheddar cheese

1½ cups soft bread crumbs
2 eggs, lightly beaten
1 tablespoon Lea & Perrins
    Worcestershire Sauce
½ teaspoon salt

In a large saucepan melt butter. Add onions; sauté until tender, about 5 minutes. Add remaining ingredients; mix well. Turn into an 8½ x 4½ x 2½-inch loaf pan. Bake in a preheated moderate oven (350 F.) until browned and hot, about 45 minutes.

COTTAGE CORN CASSEROLE
(Low Calorie)

4 eggs, lightly beaten
2 cups skim milk
1 container (12 oz.) low-fat cottage cheese
1 can (12 oz.) vacuum-packed whole kernel corn
¼ cup chopped parsley
2 tablespoons minced onion
2 teaspoons Lea & Perrins Worcestershire Sauce
½ teaspoon salt

In a large bowl combine all ingredients. Pour into a lightly buttered 1½-quart casserole. Place casserole in a larger pan. Pour hot water into the larger pan to a depth of 2 inches. Bake in a preheated slow oven (325 F.) until a knife inserted into the center comes out clean, about 1 hour and 10 minutes.

CALORIE COUNT: about 200 calories per serving.

CHEESE AND TUNA A LA PERRINS

6 servings

94

2 cans (11 oz. each) condensed Cheddar cheese soup
¾ cup beer
1 cup (4 oz.) shredded mild Cheddar cheese
2 tablespoons Lea & Perrins Worcestershire Sauce
2 cans (6 to 7 oz. each) tuna fish, drained and flaked

In a medium saucepan combine soup, beer, cheese, and Lea & Perrins. Cook and stir until mixture begins to bubble and cheese is melted. Blend in tuna; heat until hot. Serve over toast points garnished with paprika, if desired.

CHEESE AND BREAD FONDUE

6 to 8 servings

1 loaf (½ lb.) Italian bread
1 package (10 oz.) frozen mixed vegetables, thawed
2 cans (11 oz. each) condensed Cheddar cheese soup
4 eggs, well beaten
¾ cup water
3 tablespoons Lea & Perrins Worcestershire Sauce
¾ teaspoon salt

Cut bread into ½-inch thick slices. In a 2-quart casserole arrange alternate layers of bread and mixed vegetables. Combine remaining ingredients. Pour over bread mixture; cover and refrigerate for 6 hours or longer. Bake, uncovered, in a preheated slow oven (325 F.) until puffy and brown, about 1½ hours. Serve immediately.

Opposite: *Cheese and Bread Fondue*

VEGETABLE
VARIETY

Even the "I can't stand vegetables" crowd
will love these

BAKED VEGETABLE MACEDOINE   *8 to 10 servings*

1 package (10 oz.) frozen
    mixed vegetables, thawed
1 package (10 oz.) frozen
    cauliflower, thawed
1 yellow squash, thinly sliced
1 zucchini squash, thinly sliced
1 potato, peeled and diced
1 cup cherry tomatoes, halved

½ cup chopped red onion
1 cup water
¼ cup oil
2 tablespoons Lea & Perrins
    Worcestershire Sauce
1 beef bouillon cube
2 large cloves garlic, crushed
½ teaspoon Italian seasoning

Place all vegetables in an ungreased 11 x 7 x 1½-inch baking
pan. Toss gently; set aside. In a small saucepan combine remaining ingredients. Bring to boiling point; stir to dissolve
bouillon cube. Pour over vegetables. Cover tightly. Bake in
a preheated moderate oven (350 F.) until vegetables are
crisp-tender, about 1 hour, stirring once.

Opposite: *Baked Vegetable Macedoine*

BUBBLE AND SQUEAK

6 servings

¼ cup beef or bacon drippings
¼ cup chopped onion
2 cups sliced cooked potatoes
1 cup sliced cooked carrots
2 cups shredded cooked
    cabbage

2 tablespoons Lea & Perrins
    Worcestershire Sauce
Salt

In a large heavy skillet heat drippings. Add onion; sauté until tender, about 5 minutes. Add potatoes; sauté on both sides until browned. Stir in carrots and cabbage; stir-fry until vegetables are golden and "squeak" in the skillet. Stir in Lea & Perrins and salt to taste.

QUICK PEA MEDLEY

4 servings

2 tablespoons butter or
    margarine
¼ cup chopped onion
¼ cup chopped green pepper
1 package (10 oz.) frozen peas

1 can (8¼ oz.) tomatoes,
    broken up
1½ teaspoons Lea & Perrins
    Worcestershire Sauce
½ teaspoon salt

In a medium saucepan melt butter. Add onion and green pepper; sauté for 3 minutes. Add peas, tomatoes, Lea & Perrins, and salt; mix gently. Bring to boiling point. Reduce heat and simmer, uncovered, for 5 minutes.

SNAPPY GREEN BEANS

8 servings

1 can (10¾ oz.) condensed
    cream of mushroom soup
⅓ cup milk
1½ teaspoons Lea & Perrins
    Worcestershire Sauce
1 teaspoon onion powder

2 packages (9 oz. each) frozen
    French-style green beans,
    cooked and drained
⅓ cup coarsely crumbled
    corn chips

In a medium saucepan combine soup, milk, Lea & Perrins, and onion powder; cook over low heat, stirring constantly, for 5 minutes. Pour over hot green beans. Sprinkle with corn chips.

FRUITED CELERY

6 servings

1 stalk celery
3 tablespoons butter or
   margarine
⅓ cup chopped onion
1 apple, diced

½ cup golden raisins
1 tablespoon Lea & Perrins
   Worcestershire Sauce
1¼ teaspoons salt

Separate celery into ribs; cut off leaves (save for soups and stews). Slice ribs diagonally into 1-inch pieces (makes about 6 cups). In a large skillet melt butter. Add onion and celery; sauté until tender, about 5 minutes. Mix in apple, raisins, Lea & Perrins, and salt; stir-fry until celery is crisp-tender, about 5 minutes.

HOT CABBAGE SLAW
(Low Calorie)

6 servings

⅓ cup water
2 beef bouillon cubes
1 medium-sized (about 1½
   lb.) green cabbage,
   coarsely shredded
½ cup chopped onion

½ cup grated carrot
2 tablespoons wine vinegar
2 teaspoons Lea & Perrins
   Worcestershire Sauce
½ teaspoon caraway seed

In a large saucepan combine water and bouillon cubes. Bring to boiling point, stirring to dissolve bouillon cubes. Add cabbage. Reduce heat and simmer, covered, for 10 minutes. Add remaining ingredients; simmer, covered, until cabbage is tender, about 10 minutes longer.

CALORIE COUNT: about 40 calories per serving.

SQUASH SAUTE
6 servings

3 tablespoons oil
¾ pound zucchini squash, diced
¾ pound yellow squash, diced
½ cup chopped onion
1 clove garlic, crushed

1 cup diced tomatoes
1 tablespoon Lea & Perrins Worcestershire Sauce
1 tablespoon tomato paste
1 tablespoon salt

In a large skillet heat oil. Add squash, onion, and garlic; sauté for 3 minutes, stirring carefully. Combine and add remaining ingredients. Simmer, covered, until vegetables are crisp-tender, about 8 to 10 minutes, stirring occasionally.

BAKED MUSHROOM CRISP
4 to 6 servings

¼ cup butter or margarine
2½ cups (½ lb.) sliced mushrooms
2 cups croutons

1 cup light cream
1½ tablespoons Lea & Perrins Worcestershire Sauce
¼ teaspoon salt

100

In a medium skillet melt butter. Add mushrooms; sauté until golden, about 5 minutes. In a buttered 8-inch-square baking pan arrange alternate layers of mushrooms and croutons, ending with croutons. Combine cream, Lea & Perrins, and salt; pour over mushrooms and croutons. Bake in a preheated hot oven (425 F.) until top is golden brown, about 20 minutes.

POTATOES AU GRATIN
6 servings

4 cups thinly sliced peeled potatoes
¾ cup minced onions
¾ teaspoon salt
1 can (11 oz.) condensed Cheddar cheese soup

½ cup milk
1 tablespoon Lea & Perrins Worcestershire Sauce

In a well-buttered 2-quart casserole arrange potatoes, onions, and salt in alternate layers. Repeat three times. In a small saucepan heat soup along with milk and Lea & Perrins. Pour over potato mixture. Cover. Bake in a preheated moderate oven (375 F.) for 45 minutes. Remove cover and bake 15 minutes longer.

ZUCCHINI CRUNCH   *4 servings*

1 pound zucchini, sliced
1 tablespoon Lea & Perrins
  Worcestershire Sauce
4 tablespoons butter
  or margarine
Pignola nuts

In a saucepan combine all ingredients except nuts. Cook, covered, for 12 minutes. Remove to platter; sprinkle with toasted pignola nuts.

CHEESE-STUFFED POTATOES   *6 servings*

6 baking potatoes
Oil
3 tablespoons butter or
  margarine
¼ cup chopped onion
2 teaspoons Lea & Perrins
  Worcestershire Sauce
½ teaspoon salt
¾ cup shredded sharp
  Cheddar cheese

Brush potatoes lightly with oil. Place on a baking sheet; bake 101 in a preheated hot oven (400 F.) until potatoes are tender, about 1 hour. Cut potatoes in half lengthwise; carefully scoop out potato from skins. Mash potato with butter, onion, Lea & Perrins, and salt. Spoon mashed potato mixture into potato shells. Top with cheese. Return to hot oven and bake until cheese is melted, about 15 minutes. Sprinkle with paprika, if desired.

TOMATO-SHIRRED EGGS
4 servings

1 can (1 lb.) tomatoes, drained
   and crushed
2 tablespoons chopped parsley
1 tablespoon Lea & Perrins
   Worcestershire Sauce
¾ teaspoon salt, divided
8 eggs
1 tablespoon grated Parmesan
   cheese

Combine tomatoes, parsley, Lea & Perrins, and ½ teaspoon of the salt. Place in a buttered 10 x 6 x 1½-inch casserole. Form 8 wells in tomato mixture. Crack 1 egg into each well. Sprinkle with cheese and remaining ¼ teaspoon salt. Bake in a preheated moderate oven (375 F.) until eggs are set, about 10 to 15 minutes. Serve with cooked bacon or sausage, if desired.

BROILED TOMATOES
4 servings

4 tomatoes, halved
½ cup fine dry bread crumbs
¼ cup melted butter
2 teaspoons Lea & Perrins
   Worcestershire Sauce

Place tomato halves under preheated broiler; broil for 3 minutes. Combine remaining ingredients; sprinkle over tomatoes. Broil 3 minutes longer.

SAVORY SCALLOPED TOMATOES
8 servings

3 tablespoons butter or
   margarine, divided
1 cup diced celery
½ cup chopped onion
2 tablespoons flour
1 can (1 lb. 12 oz.) tomatoes
4 teaspoons Lea & Perrins
   Worcestershire Sauce
1 tablespoon sugar
1 teaspoon salt
4 slices toasted white bread,
   divided

In a medium saucepan melt 2 tablespoons of the butter. Add celery and onion; cook until tender, about 5 minutes. Blend in flour; cook and stir 1 minute. Remove from heat. Stir in tomatoes (do not crush), Lea & Perrins, sugar, and salt. Spread toast with remaining 1 tablespoon butter; cut into ½-inch cubes. Stir half of the bread cubes into the tomato mixture. Turn into a buttered 1½-quart casserole. Bake, uncovered, in a preheated moderate oven (350 F.) for 30 minutes. Top with reserved bread cubes; bake 10 to 12 minutes longer.

Opposite: *Savory Scalloped Tomatoes*

REFRESHING SALADS

Some side dishes, some main dishes,
all crisp and pretty and good

CLUSTERED BEAN AND CORN SALAD   *8 servings*

1 can (1 lb. 4 oz.) red kidney
    beans, drained
1 can (1 lb.) whole kernel
    corn, drained
1 package (9 oz.) frozen
    cut green beans,
    cooked and drained
½ cup oil

2 tablespoons Lea & Perrins
    Worcestershire Sauce
2 tablespoons wine vinegar
1 teaspoon prepared brown
    mustard
¾ teaspoon salt
½ teaspoon sugar
½ teaspoon curry powder

In a large serving bowl arrange kidney beans, corn, and green
beans in clusters; set aside. In a small container combine
remaining ingredients; mix well. Pour over vegetables. Cover
and refrigerate for 2 hours or longer. Serve on lettuce-lined
salad plates, if desired.

Opposite: *Clustered Bean and Corn Salad*

KIDNEY BEAN SALAD   *3 to 4 servings*

1 can (15 oz.) kidney beans, drained
½ cup bottled French dressing
¼ cup minced onion
1½ tablespoons Lea & Perrins Worcestershire Sauce

Combine all ingredients. Toss, cover, and chill.

FIVE VEGETABLE SALAD   *4 to 6 servings*

2 packages (10 oz. each) frozen mixed vegetables
½ cup coarsely chopped onion
6 tablespoons oil
3 tablespoons cider vinegar
1½ teaspoons Lea & Perrins Worcestershire Sauce
¾ teaspoon salt
⅛ teaspoon coarsely ground black pepper
⅛ teaspoon sugar

Cook vegetables in unsalted water following package directions. Drain. Stir in onion. Combine remaining ingredients; mix well. Pour over mixed vegetables. Cover and refrigerate at least 12 hours before serving, stirring occasionally.

MARINATED VEGETABLE SALAD   *6 to 8 servings*

1 cup bottled Italian salad dressing
3 tablespoons Lea & Perrins Worcestershire Sauce
1 package (10 oz.) frozen cauliflower, cooked and drained
1 package (9 oz.) frozen cut green beans, cooked and drained
2 cups sliced zucchini
1 green pepper, cut into strips
1 red pepper, cut into strips
1 can (3½ oz.) pitted ripe olives, drained

Combine salad dressing and Lea & Perrins; set aside. In a large bowl combine cauliflower, green beans, zucchini, green pepper, red pepper, and olives. Pour salad dressing over vegetables. Toss well. Cover and refrigerate until chilled, about 1 hour, stirring occasionally.

HOT POTATO AND EGG SALAD   *6 servings*

3 tablespoons butter or
   margarine
2 tablespoons minced onion
2 tablespoons flour
1 cup milk
1 tablespoon Lea & Perrins
   Worcestershire Sauce
1 tablespoon salt

4 cups diced, hot cooked
   potatoes
8 hard-cooked eggs, diced
1 cup thinly sliced celery
¼ cup diced green pepper
¼ cup sliced stuffed olives
¼ cup mayonnaise

In a small skillet melt butter. Add onion; sauté for 3 minutes. Stir in flour; cook and stir for 2 minutes. Blend in milk, Lea & Perrins, and salt. Cook and stir until mixture thickens, about 3 minutes. Pour over potatoes; toss well. Add eggs, celery, green pepper, and olives. Blend in mayonnaise. Sprinkle with paprika, if desired.

PICNIC POTATO SALAD   *4 servings*

4 cups chilled diced cooked
   potatoes
1 cup mayonnaise
¼ cup sliced radishes

1 tablespoon Lea & Perrins
   Worcestershire Sauce
Salt and pepper to taste

Combine all ingredients. Toss, cover, and chill.

CONFETTI EGG SALAD   *2 servings*

4 hard-cooked eggs, diced
¼ cup mayonnaise
2 tablespoons diced green
   pepper

2 tablespoons diced pimiento
2 teaspoons Lea & Perrins
   Worcestershire Sauce

Combine all ingredients. Chill.

CREAMY COLE SLAW   *4 to 6 servings*

4 cups shredded cabbage
½ cup dairy sour cream
1 teaspoon Lea & Perrins
   Worcestershire Sauce

2 teaspoons lemon juice
Salt and pepper to taste

Combine all ingredients. Toss, cover, and chill.

MOLDED CLAM AND TOMATO RING (Low Calorie)

6 servings

2 envelopes unflavored
   gelatin
½ cup cold water
1 can (10½ oz.) minced
   clams

1½ teaspoons Lea & Perrins
   Worcestershire Sauce
2¾ cups tomato juice
1 cup thinly sliced celery
¼ cup sliced scallions

Soften gelatin in water for 5 minutes. Drain clams, reserving liquid and clams separately. Add sufficient water to clam liquid to make ¾ cup. In a small saucepan heat clam liquid and Lea & Perrins just to the boiling point. Pour over gelatin; stir to dissolve. Add tomato juice. Chill until mixture thickens to consistency of unbeaten egg white. Stir in reserved clams, celery, and scallions. Pour into a 5-cup ring mold. Chill until firm. Unmold onto serving platter.

CALORIE COUNT: about 68 calories per serving.

108   CUCUMBER SALAD

3 to 4 servings

2 cucumbers, thinly sliced
½ cup bottled Italian
   dressing

1½ teaspoons Lea & Perrins
   Worcestershire Sauce

Combine all ingredients. Toss, cover, and chill.

APPLE AND VEGETABLE SALAD RING

8 servings

2 envelopes unflavored
   gelatin
½ cup cold water
2 cans (12 oz. each) ginger ale
2 teaspoons Lea & Perrins
   Worcestershire Sauce

½ teaspoon salt
1 cup diced celery
1 cup diced apple
1 cup shredded carrots

In a small saucepan sprinkle gelatin over water; let stand 5 minutes to soften. Heat over low heat to dissolve; cool slightly. In a mixing bowl combine gelatin with ginger ale, Lea & Perrins, and salt; chill until as thick as unbeaten egg white. Stir in celery, apple, and carrots. Turn into a 6-cup ring mold. Chill until firm and ready to serve. Unmold onto a serving platter. Serve with sliced cold chicken or roast beef, if desired.

FRUIT SALAD BOWL

6 servings

2 red apples, diced
1 pear, diced
1 banana, sliced
1 cup diced celery
½ cup coarsely chopped
    walnuts

Lettuce leaves
½ cup mayonnaise
2 tablespoons lemon juice
1½ teaspoons sugar
1½ teaspoons Lea & Perrins
    Worcestershire Sauce

In a medium bowl combine apples, pear, banana, celery, and walnuts; spoon into a lettuce-lined bowl. Combine remaining ingredients. Just before serving, pour dressing over salad; toss gently.

YOGURT SALAD DRESSING
(Low Calorie)

1¼ cups

2 tablespoons lemon juice
2 tablespoons catsup
2 teaspoons Lea & Perrins
    Worcestershire Sauce

¼ teaspoon garlic powder
1 cup (8 oz.) plain yogurt

In a small mixing bowl combine lemon juice, catsup, Lea & Perrins, and garlic powder; blend. Stir in yogurt. Add salt to taste, if desired. Serve over torn salad greens or mixed vegetables.

CALORIE COUNT: about 12 calories per tablespoon.

GREEN GODDESS SALAD DRESSING

2 cups

1 cup mayonnaise
½ cup dairy sour cream
1 can (2 oz.) anchovy fillets,
    drained
¼ cup chopped parsley
1 tablespoon minced onion
½ teaspoon tarragon leaves,
    crumbled

⅛ teaspoon salt
2 tablespoons wine vinegar
1 tablespoon lemon juice
1 tablespoon Lea & Perrins
    Worcestershire Sauce
1 small clove garlic

In the jar of an electric blender combine all ingredients. Blend until smooth, about 1 to 2 minutes. Serve over torn salad greens.

CAVIAR SALAD DRESSING   *about 1 cup*

½ cup dairy sour cream
¼ cup mayonnaise
3 tablespoons red caviar,
    divided
1 teaspoon onion powder

2 teaspoons catsup
1 teaspoon Lea & Perrins
    Worcestershire Sauce
½ teaspoon lemon juice

In a medium bowl combine sour cream, mayonnaise, 2 table-spoons of the caviar, onion powder, catsup, Lea & Perrins, and lemon juice. Spoon over torn lettuce; garnish with remaining 1 tablespoon caviar.

VINAIGRETTE DRESSING   *about ¾ cup*

½ cup oil
3 tablespoons vinegar
1½ teaspoons Lea & Perrins
    Worcestershire Sauce

1½ teaspoons parsley flakes
¼ teaspoon garlic powder
Salt and pepper to taste

Combine all ingredients. Toss with greens.

110

SAVORY MAYONNAISE   *about ½ cup*

½ cup mayonnaise
1 teaspoon Lea & Perrins
    Worcestershire Sauce

1 teaspoon finely chopped
    onion

Combine all ingredients. Serve over chilled vegetables or sliced tomatoes.

CALIFORNIA
SLICED VEGETABLE SALAD   *6 servings*

2 ripe avocados, peeled,
    pitted, and sliced
2 ripe tomatoes, sliced
1 red onion, thinly sliced
⅓ cup oil
1 tablespoon Lea & Perrins
    Worcestershire Sauce

1 tablespoon lemon juice
1 teaspoon basil leaves,
    crumbled
1 teaspoon salt
½ teaspoon sugar
2 tablespoons chopped
    parsley

On a shallow platter alternately arrange avocado, tomato, and onion slices, one slice overlapping the next. In a small container combine remaining ingredients except parsley. Mix well. Pour over vegetables. Cover and refrigerate for 1 hour. Sprinkle with parsley and serve.

Opposite: *California Sliced Vegetable Salad*

THIS AND THAT

A mixed bag of unusual, inventive recipes

for almost any occasion

THE SPECIAL BLOODY MARY   *four 5-ounce servings*

1 cup tomato juice
¾ cup vodka
2 tablespoons catsup
1 tablespoon lemon juice

1 teaspoon Lea & Perrins
    Worcestershire Sauce
Ice cubes
⅛ teaspoon celery salt

In a large pitcher or cocktail shaker combine tomato juice, vodka, catsup, lemon juice, and Lea & Perrins. Fill with ice cubes. Mix or shake vigorously. Strain into 6-ounce "sour" glasses. Sprinkle with celery salt.

MULLED CIDER   *about 8 servings*

2 quarts apple cider
    or juice
⅓ cup firmly packed brown
    sugar
1 cinnamon stick

⅛ teaspoon ground nutmeg
½ teaspoon Lea & Perrins
    Worcestershire Sauce
6 thin strips orange peel
¼ cup orange juice

In a medium saucepan bring cider, brown sugar, cinnamon, nutmeg, Lea & Perrins, and orange peel to boiling point. Reduce heat and simmer, uncovered, for 10 minutes. Stir in orange juice. Serve hot.

CREPES

12 crepes

2 eggs

⅔ cup milk

1 tablespoon butter or margarine, melted

½ cup all-purpose flour

¼ teaspoon salt

Oil

In a medium mixing bowl beat eggs thoroughly. Stir in milk and butter. Blend in flour and salt just until smooth. Lightly brush a 5-inch crepe pan with oil; heat over medium heat. Add 2 measuring tablespoons of the batter; tilt pan so batter covers bottom completely. Cook for 2 minutes on each side, or until golden. Repeat. Pile crepes on top of each other on a plate. Crepes may be freezer-wrapped and stored in freezer until needed.

STUFFED BAKED APPLES MERINGUE

4 servings

2 tablespoons butter or margarine, softened

½ cup raisins

⅓ cup firmly packed dark-brown sugar

½ teaspoon Lea & Perrins Worcestershire Sauce

4 medium-sized tart baking apples, cored and peeled

1 cup water

¾ cup granulated sugar, divided

2 egg whites

⅛ teaspoon cream of tartar

1/16 teaspoon salt

In a small bowl combine butter, raisins, brown sugar, and Lea & Perrins. Stuff into center of each apple. Place apples in a 12 x 7½ x 2-inch baking pan. Mix water with ¼ cup of the granulated sugar; pour over apples. Cover and bake in a preheated moderate oven (350 F.) for 30 minutes. Uncover and bake until apples are tender, about 10 minutes. Remove apples from oven; pour liquid from pan. Increase oven temperature to very hot (450 F.). In the small bowl of an electric mixer beat egg whites with cream of tartar and salt until frothy. Gradually beat in remaining ½ cup granulated sugar; beat until stiff but not dry. Cover each apple with beaten egg white mixture. Bake in a very hot oven until meringue is golden, about 3 minutes. Serve warm or cold.

JUST-BETTER GINGERBREAD

9 to 12 servings

2¼ cups all-purpose flour
2 teaspoons ground ginger
1 teaspoon salt
1 teaspoon baking powder
1 teaspoon baking soda
1 cup unsulphured molasses
¾ cup firmly packed light
    brown sugar
½ cup butter or margarine
½ cup milk
1 egg, lightly beaten
1 teaspoon Lea & Perrins
    Worcestershire Sauce
About 16 blanched whole
    almonds

In a large bowl mix flour, ginger, salt, baking powder, and soda; set aside. In a medium saucepan heat together molasses, sugar, and butter just until butter melts. Stir in milk, egg, and Lea & Perrins. Make a well in the center of the flour mixture; pour in molasses mixture; mix thoroughly until blended. Pour into a well-greased and lightly floured 9-inch square cake pan. Bake in a preheated moderate oven (350 F.) for 40 minutes. Top with almonds. Immediately return to oven; bake until a cake tester inserted in the center comes out clean, about 10 minutes longer. Cool in pan on wire rack for 10 minutes. Turn out of pan onto rack, almond side up, and cool completely. Cut into squares.

115

GRAND FINALE CAKE

12 to 16 servings

4 cups diced unpeeled apples
2 cups sugar
3 cups all-purpose flour
2 teaspoons baking soda
1 teaspoon salt
2 teaspoons ground cinnamon
1 teaspoon ground allspice
½ teaspoon ground nutmeg
½ teaspoon ground cloves
1 cup salad oil
2 eggs, lightly beaten
1 tablespoon Lea & Perrins
    Worcestershire Sauce
1 cup chopped walnuts
1 cup raisins

In a large bowl combine apples and sugar; set aside for 15 minutes. In a medium bowl sift together flour, soda, salt, and spices. Stir in oil, eggs, and Lea & Perrins. Add to apple mixture all at once; mix well. Fold in nuts and raisins. Pour into a well-greased and lightly floured 10-inch tube pan. Bake in a preheated slow oven (325 F.) for 1¼ hours. Cool in pan on wire rack for 10 minutes. Turn out of pan onto rack to cool completely.

Opposite: *Just-Better Gingerbread*

SAUSAGE 'N' RAISIN STUFFING   *about 8 cups*

2 pounds bulk pork sausage	½ cup chopped parsley
2 cups diced celery	3 tablespoons Lea & Perrins
1½ cups minced onions	Worcestershire Sauce
8 cups soft bread cubes	½ teaspoon salt
2 cups raisins	4 eggs, lightly beaten

In a large saucepan brown sausage well, about 15 minutes, stirring often. Remove meat; set aside. Pour off all but ¼ cup of the drippings from the skillet. To the drippings add celery and onions; sauté until tender, about 5 minutes. Add bread cubes, raisins, parsley, Lea & Perrins, and salt; mix well. Stir in eggs. Use to stuff a 10 to 12-pound turkey. Roast following favorite directions. Or, if desired, spoon mixture into a buttered 3-quart casserole. Bake, uncovered, in a preheated moderate oven (375 F.) until stuffing is golden, about 45 minutes.

TUNA-CHEESE MUFFINS   *6 servings*

2 cans (6 to 7 oz. each) tuna, drained and flaked	¼ cup mayonnaise
	1 tablespoon Lea & Perrins
1 cup (4 oz.) shredded sharp Cheddar cheese	Worcestershire Sauce
	6 English muffins, split
⅓ cup minced onion	

In a medium bowl mix tuna, cheese, onion, mayonnaise, and Lea & Perrins. Arrange muffin halves on a large baking sheet; top each with tuna mixture. Bake in a preheated very hot oven (450 F.) until hot and golden, about 12 minutes. Garnish with parsley, if desired.

TANGY HAM SALAD SANDWICH   *5 sandwiches*

½ cup diced celery	1 tablespoon minced onion
⅓ cup chopped walnuts	1 teaspoon Lea & Perrins
¼ cup mayonnaise	Worcestershire Sauce
¼ cup cranberry-orange relish	2 cups slivered cooked ham
	10 slices pumpernickel bread

In a medium bowl combine celery, walnuts, mayonnaise, cranberry-orange relish, onion, and Lea & Perrins. Stir in ham. Spread about ½ cup on each of 5 slices of bread. Top with remaining bread and cut in half.

SPRING SALAD SANDWICH　　　　*4 sandwiches*

1 package (8 oz.) cream
　　cheese, softened
¼ cup dairy sour cream
¼ cup chopped celery
¼ cup grated carrot

2 tablespoons chopped radishes
2 tablespoons minced scallions
1 teaspoon Lea & Perrins
　　Worcestershire Sauce
8 slices pumpernickel bread

In a small bowl thoroughly combine cream cheese, sour cream, celery, carrot, radishes, scallions, and Lea & Perrins. Spread a heaping ⅓ cup on each of 4 slices of bread. Top with remaining bread and cut in half.

PEANUT BUTTER 'N' BACON
SANDWICH FILLING　　　　*1 sandwich*

¼ cup peanut butter
2 strips crisp bacon,
　　crumbled
2 teaspoons Lea & Perrins
　　Worcestershire Sauce

2 teaspoons instant minced
　　onion
2 slices bread

Combine all ingredients. Spread on slice of bread. Top with second slice.

TARTAR SAUCE DELUXE　　　　*about 1⅓ cups*

1 cup mayonnaise
2 tablespoons minced
　　cucumber
1 tablespoon minced onion
1 tablespoon chopped pitted
　　green olives
1 tablespoon capers, drained
　　and chopped

1 tablespoon chopped parsley
1 hard-cooked egg, chopped
2 teaspoons Lea & Perrins
　　Worcestershire Sauce
1 teaspoon prepared brown
　　mustard
¹⁄₁₆ teaspoon garlic powder

In a small bowl combine all ingredients; mix well. Cover and chill. Serve with fried fish.

TASTY TARTAR SAUCE　　　　*about ½ cup*

¼ cup sweet pickle relish
3 tablespoons mayonnaise

¾ teaspoon Lea & Perrins
　　Worcestershire Sauce

Combine all ingredients. Chill. Serve with fish.

WORCESTER BUTTER SAUCE

about ⅔ cup

½ cup butter or margarine
1 tablespoon chopped parsley
2 tablespoons lemon juice
1½ teaspoons Lea & Perrins Worcestershire Sauce
⅛ teaspoon salt

In a small saucepan melt butter. Stir in remaining ingredients. Heat thoroughly. Serve hot over fish or vegetables.

CHIVE VEGETABLE BUTTER

about ½ cup

¼ cup melted butter
2 teaspoons chopped chives
½ teaspoon Lea & Perrins Worcestershire Sauce

Combine all ingredients. Serve warm over green beans, peas, or carrots.

TEXAS BARBECUE SAUCE

4 cups

1 bottle (5 oz.) Lea & Perrins Worcestershire Sauce
2 cups water
1 cup cider vinegar
¾ cup lemon juice
¼ cup oil
¼ cup firmly packed brown sugar
2 teaspoons salt
1 teaspoon garlic salt
½ teaspoon ground black pepper

In a medium saucepan combine all ingredients. Bring to boiling point. Reduce heat and simmer, uncovered, for 10 minutes. Cool. Pour into tightly covered container. This sauce will keep refrigerated for several weeks. Use for chicken, hamburgers, or steak.

A SAUCE FOR ALL BARBECUES

about 1 cup

¼ cup butter, margarine, or oil
⅓ cup firmly packed dark brown sugar
1 tablespoon onion powder
1½ teaspoons salt
1 teaspoon powdered mustard
¼ cup water
2½ tablespoons Lea & Perrins Worcestershire Sauce
1 tablespoon lemon juice

In a small saucepan melt butter. Stir in remaining ingredients. Heat until hot. Use for steak, poultry, hamburgers, or ribs.

SMACKING GOOD BARBECUE SAUCE *about 2½ cups*

¼ cup oil
¾ cup chopped onions
1 cup water
½ cup catsup
2 tablespoons Lea & Perrins
   Worcestershire Sauce

1 beef or chicken bouillon
   cube
½ clove garlic, minced

In a medium saucepan heat oil. Add onions; sauté until tender, about 5 minutes. Add remaining ingredients. Bring to boiling point. Reduce heat and simmer, covered, for 30 minutes, stirring occasionally. Use for turkey, chicken, short ribs, or hamburgers.

CRAZY BARBECUE SAUCE (But Good!) *about 1½ cups*

½ cup Lea & Perrins
   Worcestershire Sauce
½ cup catsup
½ cup strong coffee

¼ cup butter or margarine
2 teaspoons sugar
1½ teaspoons salt

In a medium saucepan combine all ingredients. Bring to boiling point. Reduce heat and simmer, uncovered, for 20 minutes, stirring occasionally. Use for roast beef, chicken, steaks, or hamburgers.

LEMON BARBECUE SAUCE *about 1 cup*

¾ cup bottled Italian
   salad dressing
¼ cup lemon juice

1 tablespoon Lea & Perrins
   Worcestershire Sauce
¼ cup minced onion

Combine all ingredients. Use for chicken, spareribs, or fish.

LONDON MUSTARD *1 cup*

1 cup prepared yellow mustard

1½ tablespoons Lea & Perrins
   Worcestershire Sauce

Blend mustard and Lea & Perrins until smooth. Spread over ham, beef, or bologna sandwiches or use in salad dressings.

SPANISH SAUCE
2 cups

2 tablespoons butter or margarine

1 cup chopped onions

2 tablespoons diced green pepper

1 teaspoon minced garlic

1 can (1 lb. 1 oz.) Italian peeled tomatoes

¼ cup chopped stuffed olives

2 teaspoons Lea & Perrins Worcestershire Sauce

1 small bay leaf

½ teaspoon sugar

½ teaspoon salt

⅛ teaspoon ground cloves

In a medium saucepan melt butter. Add onions, green pepper, and garlic; sauté until tender, about 5 minutes. Stir in tomatoes, olives, Lea & Perrins, bay leaf, sugar, salt, and cloves. Bring to boiling point. Reduce heat and simmer, partly covered, until mixture thickens, about 30 minutes, stirring occasionally. Serve hot over pork, chicken, or leftover beef.

"DELI" ONION SAUCE
1 cup

1 tablespoon oil

1 cup coarsely chopped onions

¼ cup catsup

1 tablespoon Lea & Perrins Worcestershire Sauce

⅛ teaspoon salt

In a small skillet heat oil. Add onions; sauté until tender, about 5 minutes. Do not brown. Stir in catsup, Lea & Perrins, and salt. Serve over cooked frankfurters.

PICCADILLY PICCALILLI SAUCE   *about 1¼ cups*

1 cup sweet pickle relish
2 tablespoons bottled chili sauce
1 tablespoon prepared brown mustard
1 tablespoon Lea & Perrins Worcestershire Sauce

In a small bowl combine all ingredients. Serve over cooked frankfurters or hamburgers.

CUMBERLAND SAUCE   *¾ cup*

½ cup red currant jelly
1 teaspoon sugar
1 teaspoon grated orange peel
½ teaspoon grated lemon peel
¼ cup fresh orange juice
3 tablespoons fresh lemon juice
1 teaspoon Lea & Perrins Worcestershire Sauce
2 teaspoons cornstarch
2 teaspoons cold water

In a small saucepan combine all ingredients except cornstarch and water. Stir over low heat until jelly is melted. Mix cornstarch with water; blend into sauce. Cook and stir over low heat until thickened. Serve hot over roast chicken or turkey. Or, brush over chicken parts as a glaze during last few minutes of broiling.

121

APPLESAUCE CHUTNEY   *about ½ cup*

½ cup applesauce
2 tablespoons golden raisins
¾ teaspoon Lea & Perrins Worcestershire Sauce

Combine all ingredients. Cover and chill. Serve with chicken or pork.

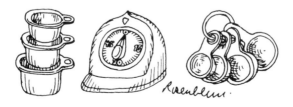

Rosenblum.

OUR MUSHROOM SAUCE   *2 cups*

2 tablespoons butter or margarine
½ cup chopped onion
1 teaspoon minced garlic
2 tablespoons flour
1 can (10½ oz.) condensed beef broth

¼ cup chopped parsley
⅛ teaspoon thyme leaves, crumbled
1 can (3 to 4 oz.) sliced mushrooms
2 tablespoons Lea & Perrins Worcestershire Sauce

In a small saucepan melt butter. Add onion and garlic; sauté for 3 minutes. Add flour; cook and stir for 2 minutes. Blend in broth, parsley, and thyme. Bring to boiling point, stirring occasionally. Reduce heat and simmer, covered, for 5 minutes, stirring occasionally. Add mushrooms and Lea & Perrins; simmer 2 minutes longer. Serve hot over steak, hamburgers, or roast beef.

122   **GROOVY GRAVY**   *about 1½ cups*

1 can (10½ oz.) beef gravy
1 tablespoon instant minced onion
1 bay leaf

½ cup water
1 teaspoon Lea & Perrins Worcestershire Sauce

In a small saucepan combine all ingredients. Bring to boiling point. Reduce heat and simmer, uncovered, for 5 minutes. Serve hot over hamburgers or leftover beef.

BURGUNDY STEAK SAUCE
A LA WORCESTER   *about 2½ cups*

2 tablespoons butter or margarine
¼ cup chopped onion
2 cans (10½ oz. each) beef gravy

3 tablespoons Burgundy or other dry red wine
4 teaspoons Lea & Perrins Worcestershire Sauce
2 tablespoons chopped parsley

In a small saucepan melt butter. Add onion; sauté for 3 minutes. Stir in gravy, wine, and Lea & Perrins. Cook and stir until hot, about 2 minutes. Stir in parsley. Serve hot over steak or hamburgers.

IDEA FINDER

Use the special index
below for quick-and-easy
meal planning.

123

124

INDEX

125

127

128